AF504818

Bible Study Guide and Workbook for Kids

A Simple and Fun Way to Discover God's Word with Lessons That Stick and Activities They'll Love

WELCOME ABOARD, CHECK OUT THIS LIMITED-TIME FREE BONUS!

Ahoy, reader! Welcome to the Ahoy Publications family, and thanks for snagging a copy of this book! Since you've chosen to join us on this journey, we'd like to offer you something special.

Check out the link below for a FREE e-book filled with delightful facts about American History.

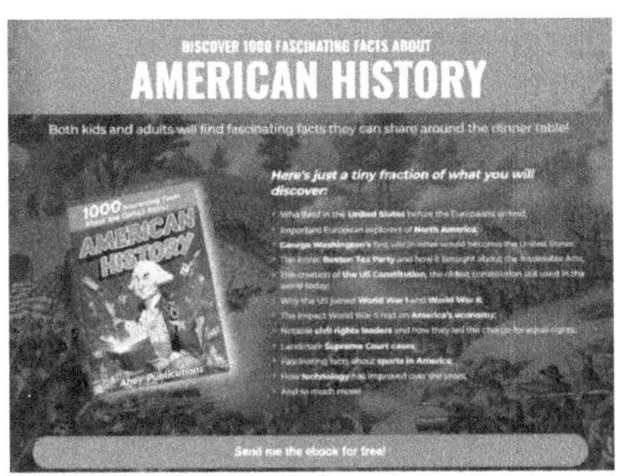

But that's not all - you'll also have access to our exclusive email list with even more free e-books and insider knowledge. Well, what are ye waiting for? Click the link below to join and set sail toward exciting adventures in American History.

Access your bonus here

https://ahoypublications.com/

Or, Scan the QR code!

Table of Contents

PART 1: BIBLE STUDY FOR KIDS

A Fun, Easy-to-Read Guide with Simple Explanations and Big Lessons to Help Kids Grow in Faith

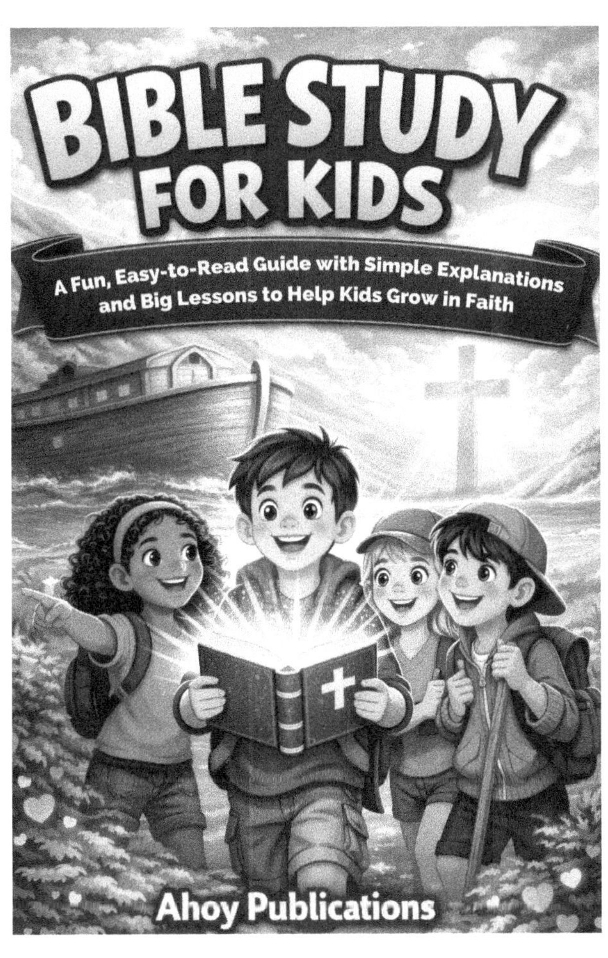

SECTION 1
DISCOVERING GOD'S TRUTH IN HIS WORD

CHAPTER 1: WELCOME TO YOUR BIBLE ADVENTURE!

Are you ready for an adventure that will take you through exciting stories, introduce you to incredible people, and help you discover the most important truths in the universe? That's what this book is all about.

This is your guide to understanding the Bible, which is **God's very own Word**. Think of it like a treasure map, and the treasure is knowing God better and growing stronger in your faith.

You might be wondering, "What is a Bible study, anyway?" It's simple: It means we're going to read parts of God's Word together, learn what they mean, and discover how God wants us to live because of what we learn. We'll explore big ideas in simple ways, and you'll find out how these stories are super important for your life today.

Here's how your adventure will work:

- ✝**Bible Stories:** We'll read exciting stories straight from God's Word.
- ✝**Simple Explanations:** We'll break down big ideas into easy-to-understand parts.
- ✝**Big Lessons:** For each chapter, we'll find one main truth, a "Big Lesson," that God wants you to learn and remember.
- ✝**Fun Activities:** You'll get to draw, write, think, and maybe even play some games. These activities will help you remember what you've learned.
- ✝**Think & Grow:** We'll have questions and ideas to help you think about how God's truths apply to your own life.

This journey is all about growing closer to God. He loves you so much, and He wants you to know Him through His Word. So, open your heart and get ready.

Key Truth for Chapter 1: Learning about God from His Word helps us understand His amazing plan and grow closer to Him.

Activity Idea: Your Bible Adventure Passport

Let's get ready. Take a moment to think about what you hope to discover in this Bible study.

1. **My Name:** ___________________________

2. **Age:** _________

3. **One thing I already know about God's Word (the Bible):**

   ____

4. **One question I have about God or His Word:**

   ____

5. **One thing I hope to learn from this Bible study:**

   ____

6. **My Bible Study Pledge:** (Put a checkmark next to each one you agree to.)

[   ] I will try my best to read and learn.

[   ] I will ask questions when I don't understand.

[   ] I will think about how God's Word can help me.

[   ] I will have fun learning about God.

CHAPTER 2: THE BIBLE: GOD'S OWN WORD

Have you ever wondered what the Bible actually *is*? It's **God's Own Word**. This means that even though human authors wrote down the words, God was working through them, making sure they wrote exactly what He wanted us to know. It's like when you tell a friend a message to write down. The words are yours, even if your friend does the writing.

The Bible is completely true and it's trustworthy.

Why is God's Word So Important?

1. **It Reveals God:** The Bible tells us *who God is*. It shows us His character: that He is loving, holy, just, powerful, and merciful.

2. **It Shows His Plan:** It explains God's plan for the world and for us, including His plan to rescue us from sin.

3. **It Teaches Us How to Live:** God's Word teaches us right from wrong and guides us on how to live in a way that pleases Him and blesses others. It's like an instruction manual for life.

How is God's Word Organized?

The Bible is a collection of 66 different books, but they all fit together perfectly. It's split into two main parts:

- ✝**The Old Testament:** This part (39 books) tells us about God's creation of the world, how sin entered, God's promises, and His relationship with His chosen people, Israel, *before* Jesus came to earth. It talks about prophets, kings, wars, and miracles.

- ✝**The New Testament:** This part (27 books) tells us all about Jesus: His birth, life, teachings, miracles, death, resurrection, and ascension. It also tells us how His followers spread the Good News and how Christians should live.

Each book in the Bible is divided into **chapters**, and each chapter is divided into smaller pieces called **verses**. This helps us find specific parts easily. For example, if someone says "Go to John 3:16," you know they mean the Book of John, Chapter 3, Verse 16.

So, when you open the Bible, you're not just reading ancient words. You're reading God's truth, His message to *you.*

Key Truth for Chapter 2: The Bible is God's inspired and unchanging Word, completely true and powerful, given to us so we can know Him.

Activity Idea: Bible Scavenger Hunt

Let's practice finding things in God's Word. Use a Bible (a physical one or an online version) to find these verses. Write down what each verse talks about.

1. **Genesis 1:1:** (Hint: First verse of the Bible.) What does it say?

____

____

2. **John 3:16:** (Hint: A very famous verse about God's love.) What does it say?

____

____

3. **Psalm 23:1:** (Hint: A popular psalm about a shepherd.) What does it say?

____

____

4. **Matthew 28:19:** (Hint: Jesus' command to His followers.) What does it say?

____

____

Extra Challenge: Can you name two books from the Old Testament and two books from the New Testament?

Old Testament:

    1. ________________

    2. ________________

New Testament:

    1. ________________

    2. ________________

CHAPTER 3: GOD, OUR INCREDIBLE CREATOR

Have you ever looked up at the stars at night? Or seen a tiny seed grow into a giant tree?

In the very first book of the Bible, Genesis, God's Word tells us the story about how everything began. It shows us that God made everything out of nothing, simply by speaking.

The Story of Creation (Genesis 1:1 - 2:3)

Imagine a time when there was nothing. No light, no land, no animals, no people, just darkness and water. Then, God's voice broke through the silence.

✝**Day 1:** God said, "Let there be light," and light appeared. He separated the light from the darkness, calling the light "day" and the darkness "night."

✝**Day 2:** God separated the waters below from the waters above, creating the sky.

✝**Day 3:** God gathered the waters together to reveal dry land. He called the dry land "earth" and the gathered waters "seas." Then, He spoke, and the earth brought forth plants, trees, and all kinds of seeds and fruits.

✝**Day 4:** God made the sun, moon, and stars to give light to the earth, to mark seasons, days, and years.

✝**Day 5:** God filled the waters with swimming creatures and the sky with all kinds of birds. He blessed them and told them to multiply.

✝**Day 6:** God commanded the earth to bring forth living creatures: livestock, creeping things, and wild animals, each according to its kind. And it was so.

But God wasn't finished. The most special part of creation happened on Day 6. **"Then God said, "Let us make mankind in our image, in our likeness, so that they may rule over the fish in the sea and the birds in the sky, over the livestock and all the wild animals, and over all the creatures that move along the ground."** (Genesis 1:26, NIV).

God created Adam and Eve in His own image. They were the first people on His Earth. He gave them the ability to think, choose, love, and care for His world. He wanted them to know and trust Him. He placed them in a beautiful garden called Eden and gave them the important job of taking care of His creation.

When God looked at everything He had made, He saw that "it was very good." (Genesis 1:31, NIV). On the seventh day, God rested from His work, setting an example for us. Now we take a day every week to rest and praise the Lord.

This story teaches us so much about God: He is all-powerful, wise, and good. He didn't *have* to create anything, but He did, out of His incredible love and goodness. And He made *you.*

You are wonderfully and purposefully made in the image of the great Creator God. He made you so that you can come to know Him. He gave you the freedom to choose love. He didn't program you like a robot, but gave you unlimited choices in life.

Key Truth for Chapter 3: God is the all-powerful and loving Creator of the universe, and He made us in His image, special and unique.

Activity Idea: Thank You, Creator God

Think about all the beautiful things God created. What are some of your favorites? Draw a picture in the space below of something God made that you are thankful for. Then, write a short prayer of thanks to God for being such an incredible Creator.

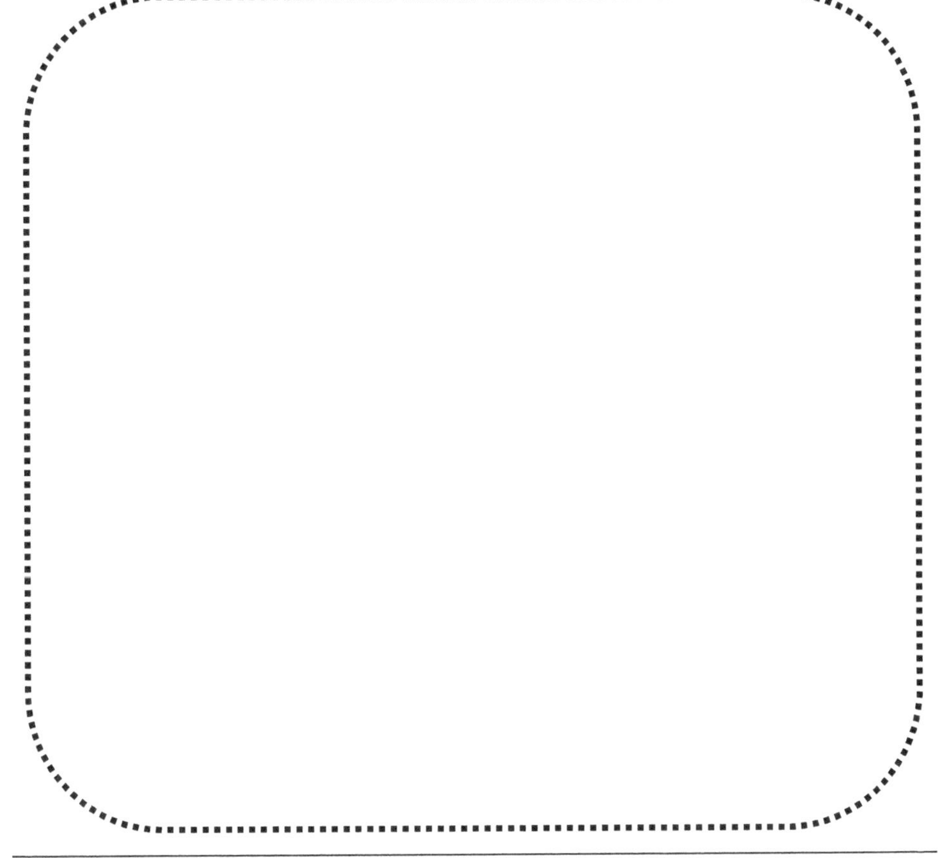

My Thank You Prayer to God: Dear God, Thank you for

____

____

____

____

____

Thank you for being my Creator and making me special. Amen.

CHAPTER 4: WHEN THINGS WENT WRONG: THE STORY OF SIN

In our last chapter, we learned that God created everything perfectly and called it "very good." He made Adam and Eve to live in a beautiful garden called Eden, where they could enjoy His presence and the world He made. Everything was perfect.

Then, something terrible happened that changed everything.

The Story of the First Sin (Genesis 3:1-24)

God had given Adam and Eve only one rule: "And the Lord God commanded the man, "You are free to eat from any tree in the garden; but you must not eat from the tree of the knowledge of good and evil, for when you eat from it you will certainly die" (Genesis 2:16-17, NIV). This rule was for their protection and to remind them that God was in charge.

One day, the cunning serpent (who was actually Satan, God's enemy, in disguise) came to Eve. He twisted God's words and asked, "Did God really say, 'You must not eat from any tree in the garden'?" (Genesis 3:1, NIV)

Eve corrected him, explaining the one rule about the tree of the knowledge of good and evil.

The serpent lied, "You will not certainly die," the serpent said to the woman. "For God knows that when you eat from it your eyes will be opened, and you will be like God, knowing good and evil." (Genesis 3:4-5, NIV)

Eve listened to the lie instead of God's clear command. She took some fruit and ate it. Then she gave some to Adam, and he ate it too.

In that moment, Adam and Eve disobeyed God. This act of disobeying God is called **sin**. Sin is when we choose our own way instead of God's way.

Immediately, their eyes *were* opened, and they realized they were naked. They made coverings for themselves from fig leaves and hid from God when He came walking in the garden.

God called out to them. Adam admitted they had eaten the fruit. Instead of taking responsibility, Adam blamed Eve, and Eve blamed the serpent.

Sin always brings sad and serious consequences. God, who is perfectly holy and just, had to respond to their disobedience.

✝The serpent was cursed to crawl on its belly.

✝Eve would have pain in childbirth and struggle.

✝Adam would have to work hard, and the ground would produce thorns and thistles.

✝And most importantly, Adam and Eve could no longer stay in God's perfect garden.

So, the story of sin reminds us that disobeying God breaks our relationship with Him and causes pain. However, it also shows us that God never gives up on His plan to rescue us and bring us back to Himself.

Key Truth for Chapter 4: Sin separates us from our holy God, but God had a plan from the very beginning to save us and bring us back to Himself.

Activity Idea: Choices and Consequences Maze

Sometimes, one small choice can lead to big consequences. Draw a maze below with the word "sadness" at the exit point. Then, run your finger along the path towards the exit, thinking about how Adam and Eve's choice led to sadness.

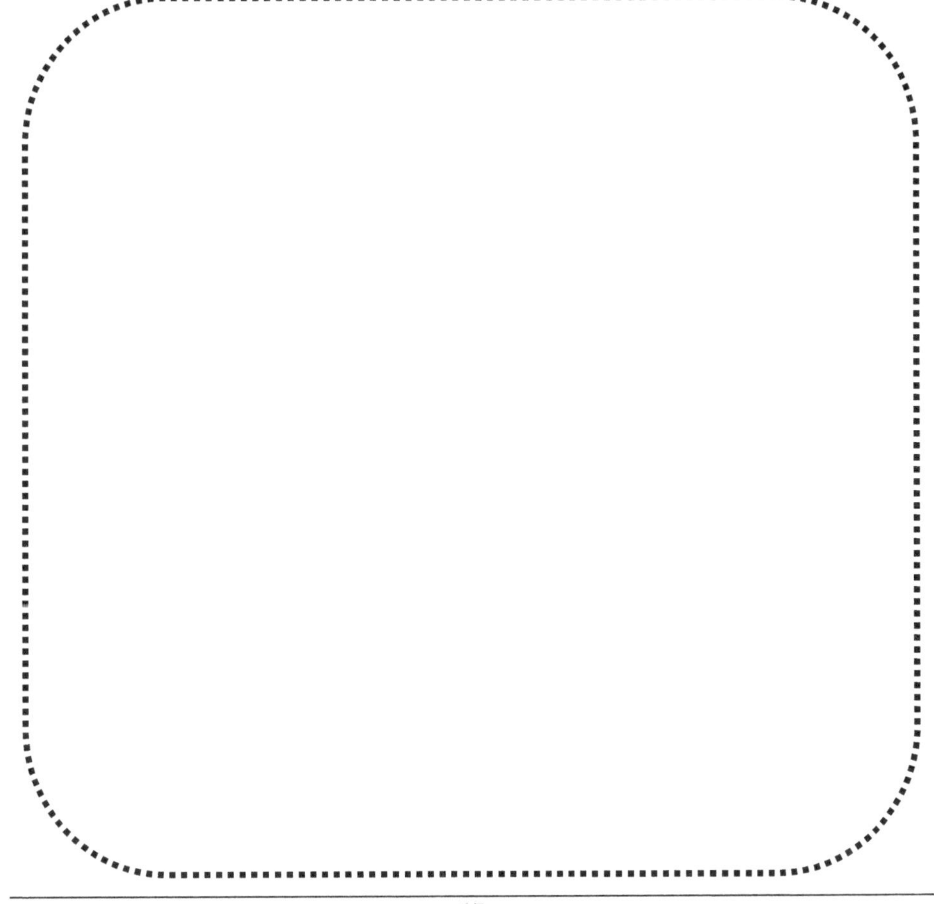

Think & Grow:

1. What was the one rule God gave Adam and Eve?

____

____

____

____

2. What is sin? (Use your own words)

____

____

____

____

3. Even after Adam and Eve sinned, what promise did God give them?

____

____

____

____

4. Why is it important for us to obey God?

____

____

____

____

CHAPTER 5: GOD'S AMAZING GRACE AND THE GREAT FLOOD: NOAH

In our last chapter, we learned how sin entered the world through Adam and Eve, causing separation from God. Sadly, after that, sin spread very quickly among people. The Bible tells us in Genesis 6:5 that the Lord saw how great the wickedness of the human race had become on the earth, and that every inclination of the thoughts of the human heart was only evil all the time. God was heartbroken by how much people had turned away from Him.

Noah Finds Favor with God (Genesis 6)

God saw that people everywhere were doing wrong. Because God is just, He decided to judge the world.. He decided to bring a great flood to cleanse the earth. There was one person, however, who stood out. His name was Noah.

The Bible says, "But Noah found favor in the eyes of the Lord." (Genesis 6:8, NIV). Noah was a righteous man, blameless among the people of his time, and he walked faithfully with God.

God spoke to Noah and told him about the coming flood. He gave Noah very specific instructions to build a huge ark, or boat. This ark was not just any boat; it was enormous. God told Noah exactly how big it should be, what materials to use, and to build different rooms inside. God also told Noah to take animals into the ark with him, along with his wife, his three sons, and their wives. They would be saved from the flood.

This command to build an ark must have seemed very strange. There had probably never been a flood like this before, and Noah lived far from any large body of water. Noah did not question God. He simply obeyed everything God commanded him to do. He spent many, many years building the ark exactly as God instructed.

The Great Flood (Genesis 7-8)

When the ark was finished, Noah, his family, and all the animals went inside. Then, God Himself shut the door. It began to rain. It rained for forty days and forty nights. Water also burst up from the ground. The waters rose higher and higher until they covered the highest mountains on Earth. Every living thing on the dry land that breathed air died, except for those safely inside the ark.

The ark floated on the waters for many months. God remembered Noah and those with him in the ark. He sent a wind to blow over the earth, and the waters began to recede. After a long time, the ark came to rest on the mountains of Ararat. Noah sent out a raven, and then a dove, to see if the water had dried up. Finally, the dove returned with an olive leaf, showing that new life was appearing.

Noah, his family, and all the animals finally came out of the ark onto dry ground. Noah's first act was to build an altar to the Lord and offer sacrifices to Him, showing his thanks and worship.

God's Promise: The Rainbow Covenant (Genesis 9)

God was pleased with Noah's worship. God then made a special promise, a **covenant**, with Noah and all living creatures. God said, "I establish my covenant with you: Never again will all life be destroyed by the waters of a flood; never again will there be a flood to destroy the earth." (Genesis 9:11, NIV).

God gave a beautiful sign to remind everyone of this promise: the **rainbow**! Whenever we see a rainbow in the sky, it is a reminder of God's faithfulness and His promise never to destroy the earth again with a flood.

The story of Noah teaches us powerful truths about God. It shows us His perfect **justice** against sin and how seriously He takes disobedience. It also shows His **grace** and **mercy** by saving Noah and his family, and His unfailing **faithfulness** to keep His promises.

Key Truth for Chapter 5: God is just and hates sin, yet He is also merciful and faithful to those who obey Him, always keeping His promises.

Activity Idea: The Ark of Safety

Draw a picture of Noah's Ark, with the animals coming out onto dry ground, and a rainbow in the sky above it. Use bright colors for the rainbow.

Think & Grow:

1. Why did God decide to send the flood?

____

____

____

____

2. How was Noah different from most other people at that time?

____

____

____

____

3. What was the special sign God gave to remind us of His promise after the flood?

____

____

____

____

4. How does Noah's Ark help us understand Jesus?

____

____

____

____

SECTION 2
GOD'S PROMISES IN THE OLD TESTAMENT

CHAPTER 6: GOD'S BIG PROMISE TO ABRAHAM

After sin entered the world, humanity became more and more rebellious against God. People started to live in their own ways, not the way of God. In His perfect plan, He decided to start over with a special family, through whom He would bring blessings to the whole world. This is where a man named **Abram** comes into our story. God would later change his name to **Abraham,** meaning "father of many nations," as part of His great promise to him.

God's Call to Abram (Genesis 12:1-3)

Abram lived in a land far away, in a city called Ur. God spoke to him one day with an amazing command and promises. God told Abram, "Leave your country, your relatives, and your father's family, and go to the land I will show you."

God did not stop there. He then made incredible promises to Abram:

✝"I will make you into a great nation."

✝"I will bless you."

✝"I will make your name great, and you will be a blessing."

✝"I will bless those who bless you, and whoever curses you I will curse."

✝"All peoples on earth will be blessed through you."

Think about that last promise. God was saying that through Abram's family, a blessing would come to *everyone* on Earth. This was a hint about Jesus, who would one day come from Abram's (now Abraham's) family line to save all people.

Abraham's Faith and Trust

Abraham faced a big decision. He had to leave everything he knew and go to a place God would only show him later. He had to trust God completely. Abraham did just that. He packed up his family, his belongings, and his nephew, Lot, and began the long journey, following God's leading. Abraham chose to believe God's promises, even though he could not see how they would happen.

Years passed, and Abraham and his wife, Sarah (who used to be called Sarai), grew very old. They still did not have any children. God had promised Abraham many descendants, as many as the stars in the sky.

Abraham might have wondered how this could ever happen. He kept trusting God. The Bible tells us that because Abraham believed the Lord, God counted it to him as righteousness. This means God declared Abraham right and good in His sight because of his faith.

God Keeps His Promises

Finally, when Abraham was 100 years old and Sarah was 90, God miraculously kept His promise. Sarah gave birth to a son, and they named him Isaac, which means "he laughs".

Later, God tested Abraham's faith in the most difficult way (Genesis 22). God told Abraham to take Isaac, his only son, to Moriah and offer him as a sacrifice. This must have been heartbreaking for Abraham. He loved Isaac deeply, and Isaac was the child through whom all of God's promises were supposed to continue.

Abraham obeyed, trusting God's wisdom and goodness. As Abraham was about to offer Isaac, an angel of the Lord called out, stopping him. God saw Abraham's faith and provided a ram caught in a thicket to be sacrificed instead.

Because of Abraham's obedience and faith, God again blessed him, "I will surely bless you and make your descendants as numerous as the stars in the sky and as the sand on the seashore. Your descendants will take possession of the cities of their enemies, and through your offspring all nations on earth will be blessed, because you have obeyed me." (Genesis 22:17-18, NIV)

This story teaches us that God is always faithful. He rewarded Abraham's faith, and through Abraham's family, God prepared the way for the greatest blessing of all: Jesus.

Key Truth for Chapter 5: God is faithful and always keeps His promises, even when we don't understand how.

Activity Idea: Promise Path

Draw a winding path starting from "Abram's Home (Ur)" and ending at "God's Promise Kept (Isaac's Birth)." Along the path, write or draw symbols for the different promises God made to Abram/Abraham and moments where he showed faith.

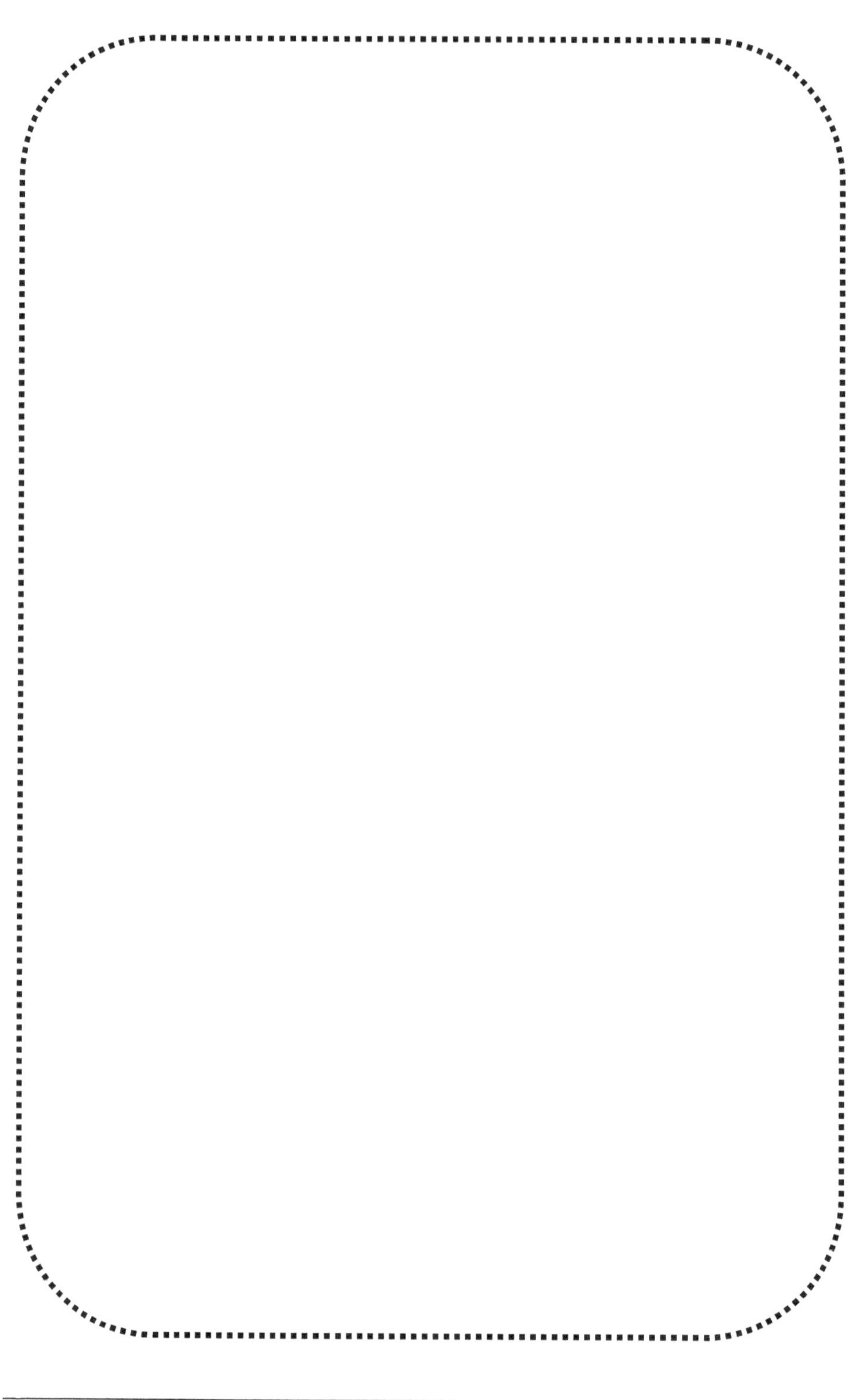

Think & Grow:

1. What was one big promise God made to Abram (Abraham)?

____

____

____

____

2. How did Abraham show that he trusted God?

____

____

____

____

3. Why is it important for us to trust God's promises today?

____

____

____

____

4. Can you think of a time when God kept a promise to you or someone you know?

____

____

____

____

CHAPTER 7: GOD RESCUES HIS PEOPLE: MOSES AND THE EXODUS

Remember how God promised Abraham that his descendants would become a great nation? Years later, Abraham's family had grown into a huge group of people called the Israelites. They had moved to Egypt, a powerful country. A new Pharaoh came to power there, and he became afraid of the Israelites' growing numbers. He forced them into cruel slavery, making their lives incredibly hard.

Moses: A Baby in a Basket (Exodus 1-2)

Pharaoh became so fearful of the Israelites that he gave a terrible command: every baby boy born to an Israelite family had to be thrown into the Nile River. It was a horrible way the Pharaoh wanted to use to ensure the babies would not survive. This was a very dark time for God's people.

An Israelite mother, however, gave birth to a beautiful baby boy. She hid him for three months, keeping him safe. When she could no longer hide him, she bravely put him in a basket and placed it among the reeds along the bank of the Nile River, trusting God for his safety. Moses's older sister, Miriam, watched from a distance to see what would happen.

Pharaoh's own daughter came down to the river to bathe. She saw the basket among the reeds and sent her servant girl to get it. When she opened the basket, she saw the baby boy crying. Her heart was filled with pity for him. She knew he was one of the Hebrew (Israelite) babies.

Miriam then stepped forward and bravely asked Pharaoh's daughter, "Shall I go and get one of the Hebrew women to nurse the baby for you?" Pharaoh's daughter agreed. Miriam quickly went and brought the baby's own mother. Pharaoh's daughter told the mother to nurse the baby for her, and she would even pay her.

So, this little baby, who was later named Moses (which means "drawn out," because he was drawn out of the water), grew up in Pharaoh's palace as if he were Pharaoh's own grandson. God had a special plan for Moses, saving him from death and preparing him to lead His people.

God Calls Moses (Exodus 3)

Years later, Moses saw an Egyptian mistreating an Israelite. He acted quickly, killing the Egyptian. Pharaoh found out, and Moses had to flee Egypt to save his life. He lived as a shepherd for many years in a faraway land. One day, God appeared to Moses in a burning bush that was not burned up. God told Moses that He had seen the suffering of His people and planned to rescue them. God sent Moses back to Pharaoh to demand freedom for the

Israelites. Moses felt scared and unsure, but God promised to be with him and give him the power he needed.

God's Mighty Power: The Plagues

Moses and his brother Aaron went to Pharaoh. They told him, "This is what the Lord, the God of Israel, says: 'Let My people go!'" Pharaoh refused to listen. He made the Israelites work even harder.

God then sent ten powerful plagues upon Egypt to show Pharaoh, and the whole world, that He alone is the true God. These were not random disasters. Each plague showed that the false gods of Egypt had no power. Each plague attacked something the Egyptians worshipped or a part of their daily life.

✝The Nile River turned to blood.

✝Frogs, gnats, and flies swarmed the land.

✝Their livestock died.

✝Painful boils covered the people.

✝Hail destroyed crops.

✝Locusts ate everything remaining.

✝A thick darkness covered Egypt for three days.

Pharaoh remained stubborn through most of the plagues. Each time he promised to let the Israelites go, then changed his mind.

The Passover: God's Protection (Exodus 12)

The tenth and final plague was the most serious. God declared He would send an angel to strike down the firstborn son in every Egyptian home. God provided a way for His people, the Israelites, to be saved. He commanded each Israelite family to sacrifice a perfect lamb and put some of its blood on the doorposts of their homes. When the death angel passed through Egypt, he would "pass over" any house marked with the lamb's blood.

This was a powerful picture. This event is called the **Passover**. It points us directly to Jesus, who is the Lamb of God. Just like the blood of the lamb protected Israel, Jesus saved us by giving His life for us. He was the ultimate sacrifice, and he did it for you.

Freedom Through the Red Sea (Exodus 14)

After the terrifying final plague, Pharaoh finally told the Israelites to leave. They rushed out of Egypt, free at last. Pharaoh quickly changed his mind again. He gathered his mighty army and chased after them. The Israelites found themselves trapped between Pharaoh's army and the vast Red Sea.

They were terrified, but God had a plan. Moses stretched out his staff over the sea, and God miraculously parted the waters. The Israelites walked across on dry ground, with walls of water on both sides. As Pharaoh's army tried to follow, God brought the waters crashing down, destroying the Egyptian army. God had powerfully delivered His people.

God Gives His Law: The Ten Commandments (Exodus 20)

God led the Israelites through the wilderness to Mount Sinai. There, God spoke directly to His people, giving them His holy laws, known as the **Ten Commandments**. These commandments were not given so people could earn their way into heaven. God had already rescued them by His grace. The laws were given to teach them how to live as His holy people, how to love Him, and how to love each other.

This journey from slavery to freedom, and receiving God's laws, showed Israel that God is mighty to save, trustworthy, and holy. He always keeps His covenant to His people. A covenant is an unbreakable bond and commitment that lasts forever.

Key Truth for Chapter 6: God powerfully delivers His people from trouble and gives us His holy law to guide us because He loves us and desires our good.

Activity Idea: Decode the Ten Commandments

God gave us these good rules to help us live. Here are some of the Ten Commandments in simpler words. Can you match the command to what it teaches us?

Commands:

1. You shall have no other gods before Me.

2. You shall not misuse the name of the Lord your God.

3. Remember the Sabbath day by keeping it holy.

4. Honor your father and your mother.

5. You shall not murder.

6. You shall not commit adultery.

7. You shall not steal.

8. You shall not give false testimony against your neighbor.

9. You shall not covet your neighbor's house.

10. You shall not make for yourself an idol.

What it Teaches Us (Match with the numbers above):

✝______ Don't want what belongs to others.

✝______ Show respect to your parents.

✝______ Worship only the one true God.

✝______ Do not take what is not yours.

✝______ Do not say bad or disrespectful things about God.

✝______ Keep special time for God to rest and worship.

✝______ Don't harm or take someone's life.

✝______ Be faithful in marriage (for grown-ups).

✝______ Don't worship statues or false gods.

✝______ Do not lie about someone.

Connect the Dots: Passover and Jesus

Draw a line from the "Passover Lamb" to "Jesus" and write one sentence about how the Passover helps us understand what Jesus did for us.

[Draw a picture of a lamb and a cross with space for text]

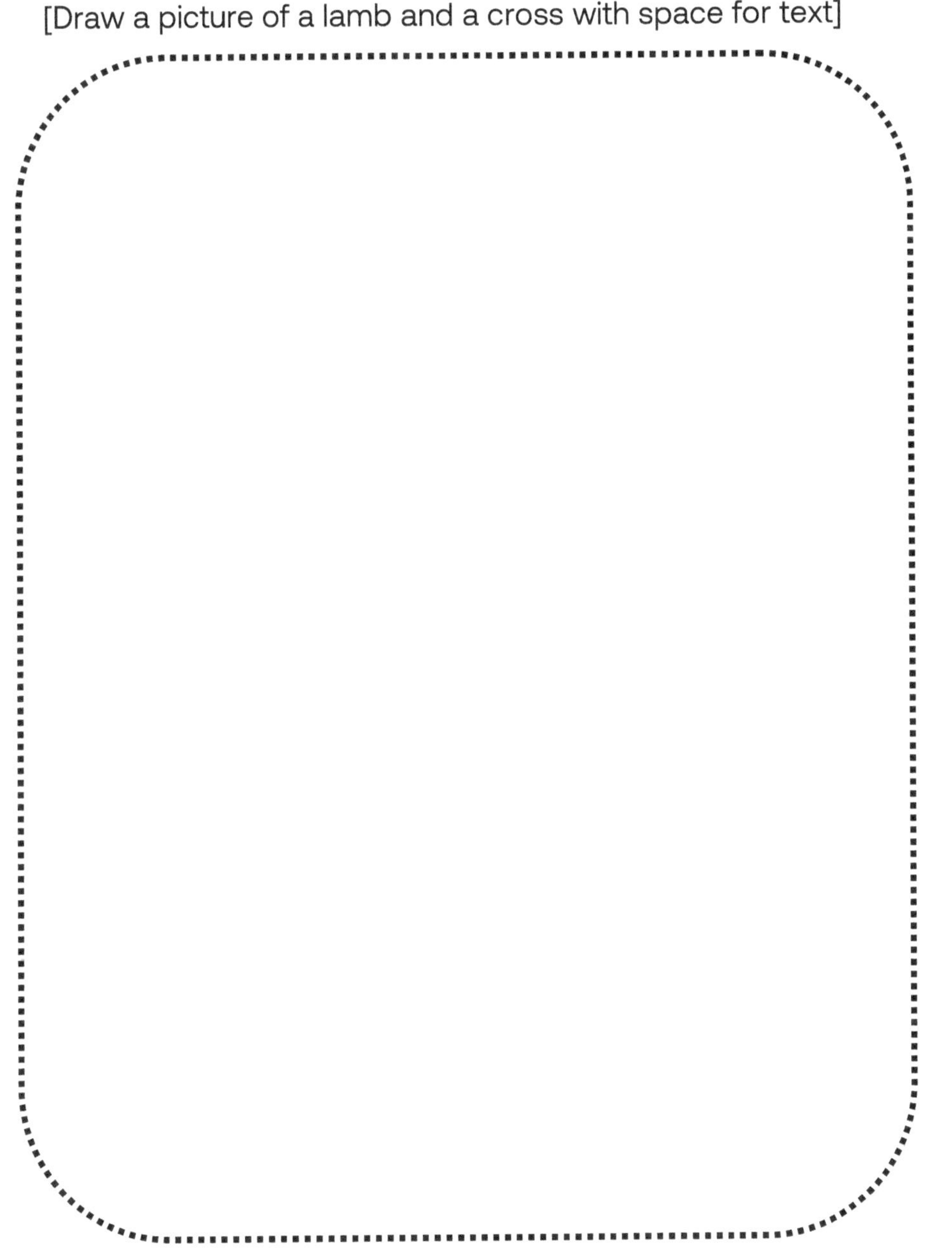

CHAPTER 8: A SHEPHERD BOY BECOMES A KING: DAVID

God had established Israel as a nation and given them His laws. The people eventually asked for a king, just like the other nations. God chose a tall, strong man named Saul to be their first king. King Saul disobeyed God, however, leading God to choose a new king. God told the prophet Samuel to go to Bethlehem to the house of Jesse, for one of Jesse's sons would be the next king.

God Chooses a King After His Own Heart (1 Samuel 16)

Samuel saw Jesse's strong, handsome sons, one by one. Each time, God told Samuel, "Do not consider his appearance or his height, for I have rejected him. The Lord does not look at the things people look at. People look at the outward appearance, but the Lord looks at the heart." (1 Samuel 16:7, NIV).

Finally, Jesse sent for his youngest son, David. David was just a boy, a shepherd. As soon as Samuel saw him, God said, "This is the one; anoint him." Samuel poured olive oil on David's head, showing that God had chosen him to be the next king. From that day on, the Spirit of the Lord came powerfully upon David.

David and the Giant Goliath (1 Samuel 17)

A terrible problem arose for Israel. Their enemy, the Philistines, had gathered for war. Their champion was a giant warrior named Goliath. He wore heavy armor and carried a huge spear. Goliath came out every day and challenged the Israelite army: "Send out a man to fight me! If he wins, we will be your slaves. If I win, you will be our slaves!"

The Israelites were terrified. King Saul himself was afraid.

And Goliath taunted the Israelites for forty days.

Young David arrived at the battlefield, bringing food for his older brothers. He heard Goliath's challenge and saw the fear in the Israelite army. David felt angry that this giant was defying the armies of the living God.

He bravely told King Saul he would fight Goliath. Saul tried to give David his own heavy armor, but it was too big. David knew he did not need heavy armor or a sword. He went to a stream, picked up five smooth stones, and took his shepherd's sling.

David faced the giant, saying, "You come against me with sword and spear and javelin, but I come against you in the name of the Lord Almighty, the God of the armies of Israel, whom you have defied. This day the Lord will deliver you into my hands, and I'll strike you down and cut off your head. This very day I will give the carcasses of the Philistine army to the birds and the wild animals, and the whole world will know that there is a God in Israel." (1 Samuel 17:45-46, NIV).

David put a stone in his sling, swung it, and hit Goliath squarely in the forehead. The giant fell to the ground! David then ran and cut off Goliath's head. The Philistines saw their champion was dead and fled in terror. God gave the victory to Israel through a courageous shepherd boy who trusted Him. David became a national hero and eventually, Israel's beloved king.

David's Sin and God's Forgiveness (2 Samuel 11-12, Psalm 51)

King David was a great king, leading Israel and worshipping God. He was known as a "man after God's own heart." Even good people, however, can make bad choices. One day, David stayed home from battle.

He saw a woman named Bathsheba, and he sinned by taking her to be with him, even though she was married. David then arranged for her husband, Uriah, a loyal soldier, to be killed in battle to cover up his sin.

God sent the prophet Nathan to confront David with his sin. Nathan told David a story about a rich man who stole a poor man's only lamb. David became very angry, saying the rich man deserved to die. Nathan then pointed at David and said, "You are the man!"

David immediately recognized his sin. He was heartbroken and truly sorry. He cried out to God in repentance, saying, "I have sinned against the Lord." He later wrote Psalm 51, a prayer asking for God's forgiveness and a clean heart.

God is holy and just, so David's sin had serious consequences for his family and kingdom. God is also merciful and forgiving. Because David genuinely confessed his sin and turned back to God, God forgave him. This shows us that God will always forgive us when we truly confess our sins and turn away from them. Even though we mess up, God is ready to offer His grace and a new start.

Key Truth for Chapter 7: God sees our hearts, uses even our weaknesses for His glory, and graciously forgives us when we turn back to Him.

Activity Idea: Heart Check

Remember what God told Samuel: "People look at the outward appearance, but the Lord looks at the heart."

1. What are some "outward appearances" people might see about you? (e.g., your clothes, your hair, how tall you are, if you're good at sports).

____

____

____

____

2. What are some things God sees in your heart? (e.g., your thoughts, your feelings, if you love Him, if you try to obey Him, if you're kind).

____

____

____

____

SECTION 3
THE GOOD NEWS OF JESUS

CHAPTER 9: GOD'S GREATEST GIFT: JESUS IS BORN!

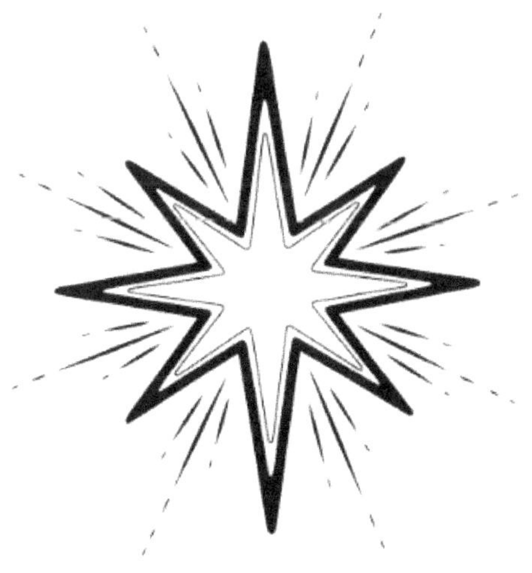

We have explored many incredible stories from the Old Testament: Creation, the spread of sin, God's justice in the flood, His promise to Abraham, His mighty rescue of Israel through Moses, and His faithfulness to David.

All these stories, in different ways, were pointing to something even greater to come. They were like hints or puzzle pieces waiting for the final, most important piece.

God Sends His Son (Matthew 1:18-25, Luke 2:1-20)

Hundreds of years after David, God would send His promised Savior. This Savior would be unlike any other. He would be God's own Son, born into the world.

God chose a young woman named Mary to be the mother of this special child. Mary was a virgin, meaning she had never been married or had children. She was betrothed to marry Joseph, who would become her husband.

An angel named Gabriel appeared to her and told her she would have a baby boy through the power of the Holy Spirit.

An angel also appeared to Joseph in a dream with the following message: "Joseph son of David, do not be afraid to take Mary home as your wife, because what is conceived in her is from the Holy Spirit. She will give birth to a son, and you are to give him the name Jesus, because he will save his people from their sins (Matthew 1:20-21, NIV).

A special decree from the Roman Emperor Caesar Augustus made everyone travel to their hometowns to be counted for taxes. Joseph and Mary, who was very pregnant, had to travel a long way from Nazareth to Bethlehem, the town of David. When they arrived, the town was so crowded that there was no room for them anywhere, not even at the inn. They had to stay in a stable, a place where animals lived.

While they were there, Mary's baby was born. She wrapped her baby, Jesus, in cloths and laid Him gently in a manger, which was a feeding trough for animals.

On a hillside nearby, shepherds were watching their sheep. Suddenly, an angel of the Lord appeared to them, and the glory of the Lord shone around them. The shepherds were terrified. The angel told them, "Do not be afraid. I bring you good news that will cause great joy for all the people. Today in the town of David a Savior has been born to you; he is the Messiah, the Lord." (Luke 2:10-11, NIV). The angel explained they would find the baby wrapped in cloths and lying in a manger.

Suddenly, a huge crowd of angels appeared, praising God and saying, "Glory to God in the highest heaven, and on earth peace to those on whom His favor rests!"

The shepherds quickly went to Bethlehem and found Mary, Joseph, and the baby Jesus, just as the angel had told them. They told everyone what they had seen and heard. Everyone who heard their story was amazed.

Wise Men Worship the King (Matthew 2:1-12)

News of this special King spread far and wide. Wise men from the East, who studied the stars, saw a unique star that indicated the King of the Jews had been born. They traveled a long distance, following this star, all the way to Jerusalem. There, they began asking, "Where is the one who has been born king of the Jews? We saw His star when it rose and have come to worship Him."

King Herod, the current ruler, heard this and became very troubled. He secretly called the wise men and found out from them the exact time the star had appeared. He then sent them to Bethlehem, saying, "Go and search carefully for the child. As soon as you find him, report to me, so that I too may go and worship him." (Matthew 2:7, NIV)

The wise men continued to Bethlehem, guided by the star, which stopped over the place where the child was. They were filled with joy.

They bowed down and worshipped Him, offering Him precious gifts: gold (fit for a king), frankincense (a special incense used in worship, fit for God), and myrrh (a spice used for burial).

After their visit, God warned the wise men in a dream not to return to Herod, so they went back to their country by another route.

Jesus' birth was the moment God's biggest promise began to truly unfold. It was the beginning of God's rescue plan for all humanity. Jesus came to earth to teach us about God, and to make a way for us to be forgiven of our sins and have a relationship with God forever.

Key Truth for Chapter 9: Jesus is God's promised Savior, sent to earth as a baby to rescue us from sin and bring us eternal life.

Activity Idea: Draw the Nativity Scene

Use the space below to draw your own picture of the Nativity, showing Baby Jesus in the manger, Mary and Joseph, and some shepherds or angels.

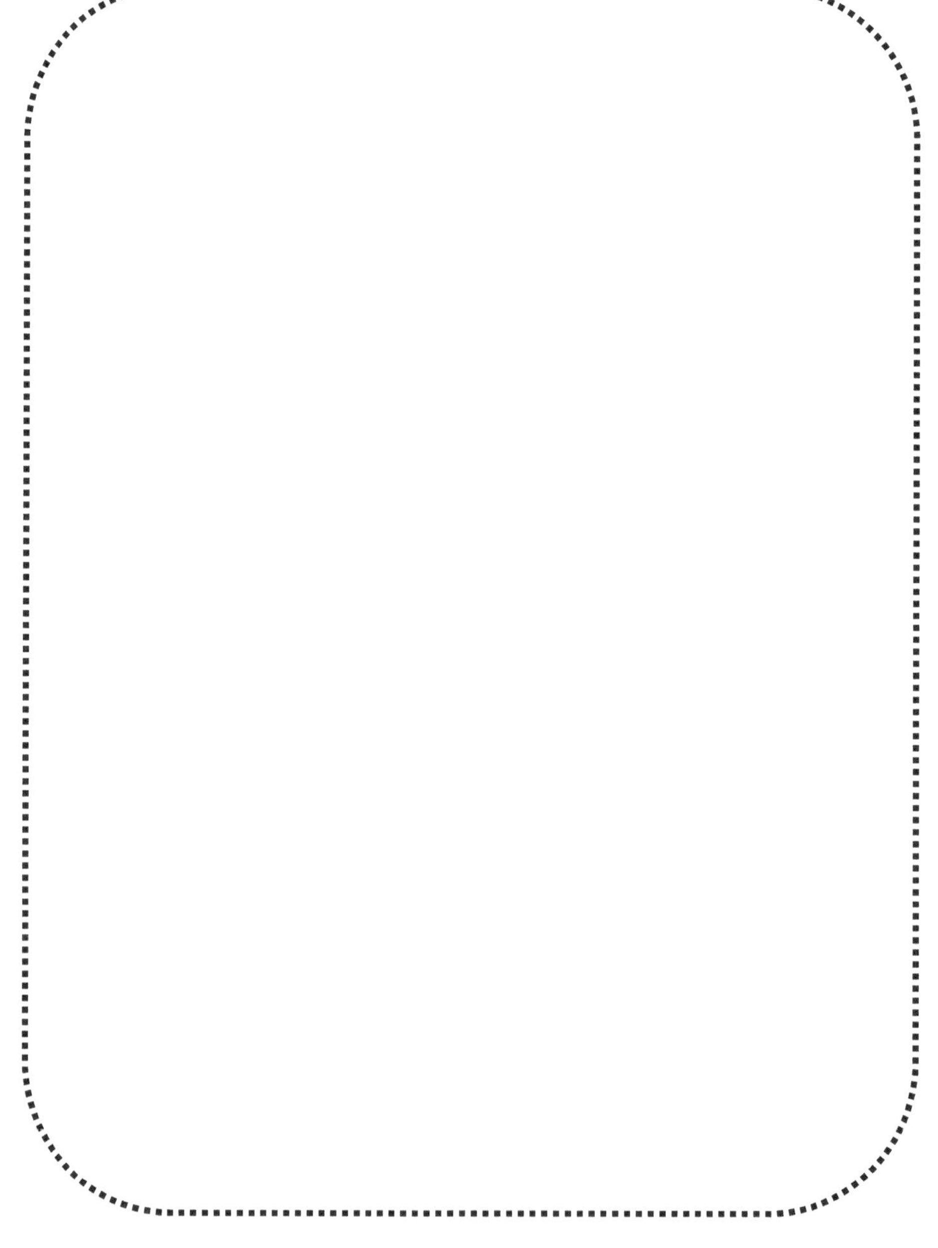

CHAPTER 10: JESUS SHOWS US GOD'S LOVE

Jesus grew up in the town of Nazareth. He learned and became strong, filled with wisdom. God's favor was on Him (Luke 2:52). When He was about 30 years old, Jesus began His special work, called His ministry.

For about three years, Jesus traveled around, teaching people about God's Kingdom and showing them who God truly is. He did two main things: He performed miracles, and He taught powerful lessons. Both showed us God's incredible love and power.

Jesus Heals and Forgives: The Paralyzed Man (Mark 2:1-12)

One day, Jesus was teaching in a house in Capernaum. So many people crowded around the door that there was no room left, not even outside. Four men carried their friend, who could not walk on a mat. They desperately wanted Jesus to heal him. They could not get through the crowd.

The men did not give up. They had an idea. They carried their friend to the roof of the house. They carefully dug a hole through the roof above where Jesus was teaching. Then, they gently lowered their friend on his mat right down in front of Jesus.

Jesus saw their great faith. He did not immediately say, "Get up and walk!" Instead, He looked at the paralyzed man and said, "Son, your sins are forgiven."

Some religious teachers sitting there thought, "Who can forgive sins? Only God can do that!" Jesus knew what they were thinking. He said to them, "Which is easier: to say to this paralyzed man, 'Your sins are forgiven,' or to say, 'Get up, take your mat and walk'?"

Jesus then told them, "I want you to know that the Son of Man has authority on earth to forgive sins." He turned to the man and commanded, "I tell you, get up, take your mat and go home."

Immediately, the man stood up, took his mat, and walked out right in front of everyone! The crowd was amazed and praised God, saying, "We have never seen anything like this!" This miracle showed Jesus' power over sickness and, even more importantly, His divine power to forgive sins.

Jesus Teaches About God's Love: The Lost Son (Luke 15:11-32)

Jesus also taught people through stories called **parables**. Parables are like earthly stories with heavenly meanings. They help us understand big truths about God's Kingdom. Here is one of His most famous parables:

Jesus told a story about a man who had two sons. The younger son told his father, "Father, give me my share of the inheritance." This was a very disrespectful thing to ask, as it meant he wished his father were already dead! The loving father, however, divided his property between his two sons.

The younger son quickly gathered all his money and traveled to a faraway country. There, he wasted all his money on foolish and wild living. A terrible famine (a time when there was no food) came to that land, and the young man became very poor. He was so desperate that he got a job feeding pigs, which was a very shameful job for a Jewish person. He was so hungry, he even wanted to eat the pods the pigs were eating.

Finally, he came to his senses. He thought, "My father's hired servants have more than enough food, and here I am starving to death! I will go back to my father and say to him, 'Father, I have sinned against heaven and against you. I am no longer worthy to be called your son; make me like one of your hired servants.'"

He started his long journey home. While he was still a long way off, his father saw him. The father's heart was filled with compassion! He ran to his son, threw his arms around him, and kissed him.

The son started his prepared speech, "Father, I have sinned against heaven and against you. I am no longer worthy..." The father did not let him finish. He immediately told his servants, "Quick! Bring the best robe and put it on him. Put a ring on his finger and sandals on his feet. Bring the fattened calf and kill it. Let's have a feast and celebrate. This son of mine was dead and is alive again; he was lost and is found!" And so, they began to celebrate.

Meanwhile, the older brother was in the field working. As he approached the house, he heard music and dancing. He became angry when he learned his wasteful brother was being celebrated. His father went out to plead with him, explaining, "My son, you are always with me, and everything I have is yours. We had to celebrate and be glad, because this brother of yours was dead and is alive again; he was lost and found."

This parable teaches us about God's incredible love and forgiveness. The father represents God, and the lost son represents anyone who turns away from God through sin. God is always watching, waiting, and ready to welcome us home with open arms when we turn from our wrong ways and come back to Him. He celebrates when we return.

Both Jesus' powerful miracles and His loving teachings perfectly show us who God is. He is full of power, wisdom, and an endless supply of love for us.

Key Truth for Chapter 10: Jesus is God incarnate, perfectly demonstrating God's power, love, and truth through His life and teachings.

Activity Idea: Parable Power

The Parable of the Lost Son teaches us that God is ready to forgive.

What did the younger son do that was wrong?

____

____

____

How did the father show he loved his son, even when the son had messed up?

____

____

____

What does this parable teach you about how God feels when we mess up and then turn back to Him?

____

____

____

Show God's Love

Think of some ways Jesus showed love to people in the stories you know (healing, teaching, forgiving). List two ways here:

____

____

____

Now, think of one way *you* can show God's love to someone this week. My plan:

CHAPTER 11: JESUS SAVES US: THE CROSS AND THE EMPTY TOMB

We have seen how Jesus came to earth, born as a baby, and how He showed God's love through His powerful miracles and wise teachings. Every miracle and every parable pointed to one big reason why Jesus came: to rescue us from our sins and bring us back to God. This rescue mission required the greatest act of love and sacrifice ever known.

The Cross: Jesus' Sacrifice for Sin (Matthew 27)

Religious leaders in Jerusalem felt jealous of Jesus and did not believe He was the Son of God. They arrested Him and put Him on an unfair trial. People shouted for Him to be crucified, a very painful way of dying that was common at that time.

Jesus, though innocent, allowed Himself to be nailed to a cross. He suffered terribly there. He was not just suffering physical pain; He was taking the punishment for every wrong thing you and I have ever done, or will ever do. He carried the weight of the world's sin. As He hung on the cross, the sky became dark for three hours. Jesus cried out, "It is finished!" and then He died. He gave His life willingly, out of unimaginable love for us.

Jesus' body was taken down from the cross and placed in a tomb, a cave-like grave, cut out of rock. A large stone was rolled in front of the entrance, and guards were placed there to make sure no one could steal His body. It seemed like the story had ended in sadness.

The Empty Tomb: Jesus Conquers Death (Matthew 28, Luke 24)

A miraculous event took place on the third day after Jesus' death. Early on Sunday morning, some women who loved Jesus went to the tomb to prepare His body. They wondered who would roll away the heavy stone for them. As they arrived, they saw that the stone had already been rolled away.

An angel of the Lord sat on top of it. His clothes were white as snow. The guards were so terrified they fainted.

The angel told the women, "Do not be afraid, for I know that you are looking for Jesus, who was crucified. He is not here; He has risen, just as He said!" The angel invited them to see the empty place where Jesus' body had been. The women ran quickly to tell Jesus' disciples the Good News.

Jesus had truly risen from the dead. This proved that He is indeed the Son of God. It showed He had complete power over sin, death, and even the grave itself. Over the next 40 days, Jesus appeared to His disciples and many other people, showing them He was alive. He taught them more about God's Kingdom.

The Ascension: Jesus Returns to Heaven (Acts 1:6-11)

Forty days after His resurrection, Jesus gathered His disciples on a mountain. He gave them a final instruction to go into all the world and share the Good News about Him. Then, as they watched, Jesus was lifted up into the sky. A cloud took Him out of their sight. Two angels stood nearby and told the disciples that Jesus would return in the same way He left.

Jesus is now in heaven, sitting at the right hand of God the Father. He is reigning as King, and He is preparing a place for all who believe in Him. His ascension means He is powerfully ruling and will one day return to gather His people and make all things new.

Jesus' death, resurrection, and ascension are the most important events in history. His death paid the penalty for our sins. His resurrection means He conquered death and offers us new, eternal life. His ascension means He is our reigning King who will come back for us. This is the amazing Good News of Jesus.

Key Truth for Chapter 11: Jesus died on the cross to pay the penalty for our sins and rose again, defeating death, so that all who believe in Him can have forgiveness and eternal life with God.

Activity Idea: The Empty Tomb

Draw a picture of the empty tomb on Easter morning. You can include the stone rolled away, angels, or the amazed women. What do you think it felt like to see that empty tomb?

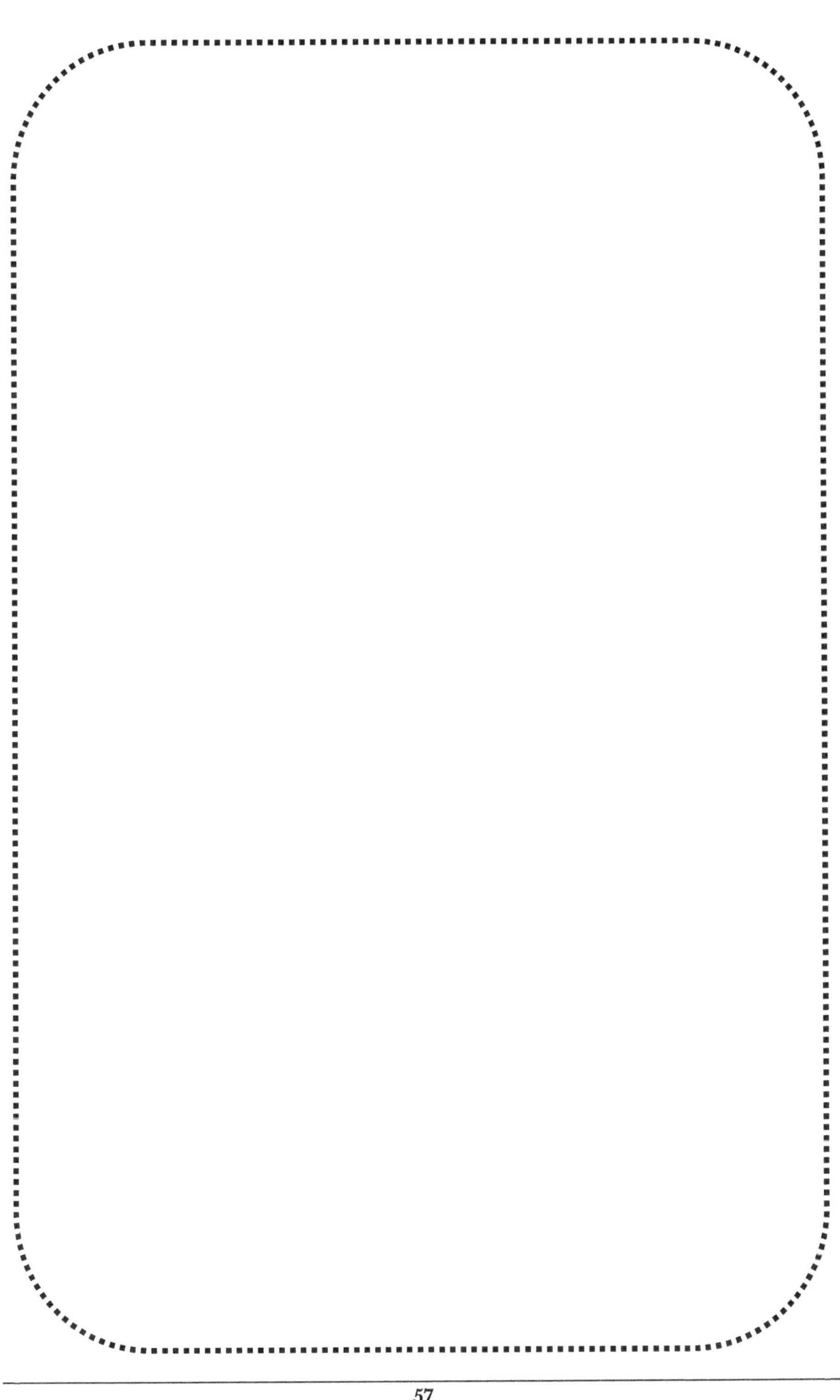

What Does It Mean for You?

Jesus died and rose again for *you!*

1. Because Jesus died on the cross, what can you receive?

____

____

____

____

2. Because Jesus rose from the dead, what hope do you have?

____

____

____

____

SECTION 4
LIVING FOR GOD

CHAPTER 12: TALKING WITH GOD: PRAYER AND HIS WORD

We have learned that God created us, that sin separated us from Him, and that Jesus came to rescue us by dying for our sins and rising again. Now that Jesus has made a way for us to have a relationship with God, how do we actually *do* that?

It is like any friendship. You build a friendship by spending time together, talking, and listening. Our relationship with God works the same way. We talk to God through **prayer**, and we listen to God when we read His **Word**, the Bible.

Talking to God: Prayer

What is prayer? Prayer is simply talking to God. He is always ready and willing to listen to you, no matter where you are or what time it is. You do not need special words or to be in a special place. You can talk to Him in your heart, out loud, kneeling, standing, or even running.

What can you pray about? Anything!

✝**Thank Him:** Thank God for His love, for Jesus, for your family, for nature, for food, for anything good in your life. (Psalm 107:1)

✝**Tell Him Your Worries:** Share your fears, your struggles, or anything that makes you sad or anxious. God cares about everything that concerns you. (Philippians 4:6)

✝**Ask for Help:** Ask God for wisdom when you need to make a choice, for strength when you are weak, or for help for yourself and others. (Matthew 7:7)

✝**Say Sorry:** When you mess up or sin, you can tell God you are sorry, just like David did. He promises to forgive you. (1 John 1:9)

✝**Pray for Others:** Ask God to help your family, friends, teachers, or anyone you know who needs Him. This is called interceding. (1 Timothy 2:1)

God is never too busy to hear you. He loves it when His children talk to Him.

Listening to God: His Word (The Bible)

God wants to talk to us too! He speaks to us through His inspired Word, the Bible. The Bible is not just an old book; it is God's living message to you.

Why should you read the Bible?

✝**To Know God:** The Bible is how we learn about God's character, His plans, His love, and His power.

✝**To Know His Will:** It teaches us how God wants us to live, what pleases Him, and what helps us make good choices.

✝**To Get Wisdom:** It gives us guidance, comfort, and strength for every situation in life. (Psalm 119:105)

✝**To Grow in Faith:** The more you read about God, the more you will trust Him and grow closer to Him.

How can you read the Bible? You do not have to read a whole book at once. You can start with a few verses each day. Maybe begin with a book like John in the New Testament to learn more about Jesus, or the Psalms for powerful prayers, or Proverbs for wise advice. You can also ask your parents or a trusted adult to help you find good parts to read. When you read, ask the Holy Spirit to help you understand what God wants you to learn.

Building a Relationship with God

Prayer and reading God's Word work together like two sides of a conversation. You talk to God, and God talks to you. When you do both regularly, your relationship with God will grow stronger and stronger. He wants to know you personally, and He wants you to know Him deeply.

Key Truth for Chapter 12: God desires a personal relationship with us, and we build this relationship by talking to Him in prayer and listening to Him through His Word.

Activity Idea: My Prayer & Bible Bites Journal

It is a great idea to keep track of your prayers and what you learn from God's Word. Here is a simple journal template you can use:

My Prayer & Bible Bites Journal

Date: __________________

My Prayer to God (What I want to talk to Him about):

____

____

____

Bible Bite! (What I read today):

Book: _____________________________

Chapter: _____________________________

Verse(s): _____________________________

What I learned from God's Word today:

____

____

____

How I can apply this to my life:

____

____

____

My Favorite Bible Verse Drawing:

Choose one Bible verse you really like. Write it out here, and then draw a picture that helps you remember it.

My Favorite Verse:

____

____

____

____

CHAPTER 13: GROWING IN FAITH: OBEYING, LOVING, AND SHARING

You have learned so much in this Bible adventure. You know that God is our Creator, that sin separated us from Him, and that Jesus came to rescue us. You also know that you can talk to God and listen to Him through His Word. This is how we begin to know God. What happens next? We start to grow in our faith.

Growing in faith means becoming more and more like Jesus. It is not just about knowing *about* God in your head; it is about living *for* God with your whole heart, every single day. The Holy Spirit, who lives in everyone who trusts Jesus, helps us do this. The Holy Spirit gives us power and guidance to grow in three important ways: by obeying God, by loving others, and by sharing the Good News of Jesus.

1. Obeying God's Word

Why should we obey God? We obey God not to earn His love or get to heaven. We obey God because we *love* Him and want to please Him. It shows our thankfulness for His gift of salvation.

God's commands, like the Ten Commandments and all of Jesus' teachings, are always good. They are like instructions from a loving Parent who knows what is best for us. Obeying God keeps us safe, helps us live wisely, and brings joy. The Holy Spirit gives us the strength to choose what is right, even when it is hard.

2. Loving Others

Jesus gave us a very clear command: "Jesus replied: "'Love the Lord your God with all your heart and with all your soul and with all your mind.' This is the first and greatest commandment. And the second is like it: 'Love your neighbor as yourself." (Matthew 22:37-39, NIV). God showed us the greatest love by sending Jesus. We can show our love for God by loving the people around us.

How can you show love to others?

- **Be kind:** Use kind words, offer a helping hand, or give a cheerful smile.
- **Forgive others:** Everyone makes mistakes. Choose to forgive those who hurt you, just as God forgives you.
- **Share:** Share your toys, snacks, or even your time with someone who needs it.
- **Be patient:** Show patience with your family and friends, even when things get difficult.
- **Listen:** Really listen when someone is talking to you.
- **Help out:** Do chores without being asked, or offer to help someone with a task.

When you love others, you are showing them God's love, and that is a beautiful thing.

3. Sharing the Good News

Imagine you found the best news ever, maybe a secret map to a treasure or a cure for all sickness. Would you keep it to yourself? Of course not! You would want to share it with everyone.

The Good News about Jesus is the best news in the whole world! Everyone needs to hear that God loves them, that Jesus died for their sins, and that they can have eternal life with Him. You can be a part of sharing this news.

How can you share the Good News?

- ✝**Live by example:** Let people see Jesus in you through your kindness, joy, and peace.
- ✝**Tell your story:** Share what God has done for you and how Jesus has changed your life. You do not need to know everything; just share what you know.
- ✝**Invite a friend:** Invite a friend to Sunday school, church, or a Christian club where they can learn more about Jesus.
- ✝**Answer questions:** If someone asks you about your faith, try to answer honestly and gently.

Sharing Jesus does not have to be scary. You are simply telling people about the greatest friend you have.

Growing in faith is a lifelong journey. You will keep learning and changing as you follow Jesus. God is with you every step of the way, helping you to obey, to love, and to share His incredible Good News.

Key Truth for Chapter 13: When we trust Jesus, the Holy Spirit helps us grow more like Him, so we can obey God, love others, and share His Good News with the world.

Activity Idea: Love in Action Checklist

How can you show God's love this week? Check off the boxes as you do these things, or write in your own ideas!

✝[ ] Help a parent or guardian with a chore without being asked.

✝[ ] Say a kind word to someone who looks sad.

✝[ ] Share something (a toy, a snack, a drawing) with a sibling or friend.

✝[ ] Forgive someone who upset you.

✝[ ] Listen carefully when someone is talking.

✝[ ] Pray for a friend or family member.

✝[ ] **My own idea:** _______________________________________

✝[ ] **My own idea:** _______________________________________

Sharing Jesus with the World

Draw a picture of yourself sharing the Good News of Jesus. This could be you talking, being kind, inviting someone, or anything that shows you living for Jesus.

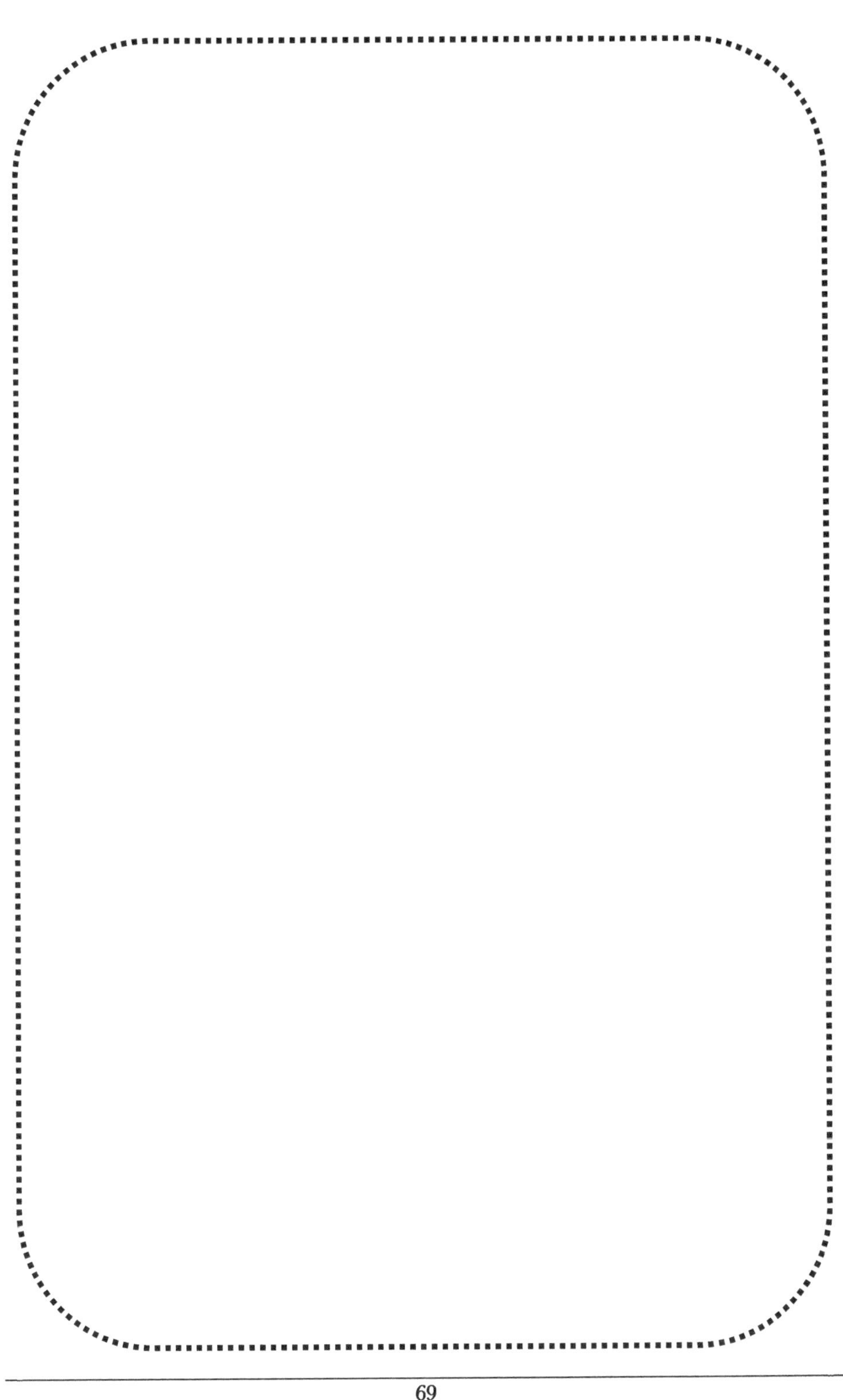

CHAPTER 14: YOUR FOREVER FRIEND: WALKING WITH JESUS

Wow! You have come so far on this Bible adventure. You have learned about God's creation, how sin messed things up, and God's incredible plan to send Jesus to rescue us. You know how to talk to God through prayer and listen to Him through His Word. You also understand how to grow in your faith by obeying, loving, and sharing.

Now, it is important to remember that this is the beginning of a great journey. Your relationship with God, through Jesus, is a forever journey. Jesus is not just a historical figure or a powerful Savior. He is your **Forever Friend**.

Jesus: Always with You

Think about your best friend. You love spending time with them, talking to them, and doing things together. Jesus wants that kind of relationship with you, only even deeper and more special.

☩**He is always with you:** Jesus promised His disciples, "I am with you always, to the very end of the age." (Matthew 28:20). He is with you when you are happy, when you are sad, when you are playing, and when you are trying to sleep. You are never alone.

☩**He understands you:** Jesus lived as a human being. He experienced hunger, tiredness, joy, and even sadness. He understands your feelings and what you go through. (Hebrews 4:15).

☩**He guides you:** Jesus wants to help you make good choices and live a life that honors God. He will guide you through His Holy Spirit, through His Word, and sometimes even through wise people around you. (Psalm 32:8).

☩**He helps you:** When you face difficult things, or when you feel weak, Jesus gives you strength. You can do all things through Him who gives you strength. (Philippians 4:13).

☩**He loves you unconditionally:** There is nothing you can do to make Jesus love you more, and nothing you can do to make Him love you less. His love is perfect and never fails. (Romans 8:38-39).

The Journey Continues

Walking with Jesus is an ongoing adventure. You will keep learning new things about God every day. You will face new challenges, however, you will also experience new joys.

Keep doing the things you have learned in this book:

⸸Keep talking to God in prayer.

⸸Keep reading His Word, the Bible.

⸸Keep choosing to obey Him in the big and small things.

⸸Keep loving others with His love.

⸸Keep sharing the Good News about Jesus with your words and actions.

You will fall down sometimes, everyone does. A forgiving God is always ready to pick you up and help you try again. He is patient and kind.

Your Forever Hope: Heaven and Jesus' Return

The best part of walking with Jesus is the incredible hope we have for the future. Jesus went to heaven after He rose from the dead. He is not just "gone"; He is there right now, preparing a place for all who believe in Him. He said, "And if I go and prepare a place for you, I will come back and take you to be with me that you also may be where I am." (John 14:3, NIV).

One day, Jesus will return to earth. He will come back for His people, and we will be with Him forever in heaven. There will be no more sadness, no more pain, only perfect joy and perfect peace in God's presence.

So, trust Jesus with your whole heart. Lean on Him. Talk to Him. Listen to Him. Enjoy every step of this incredible, forever adventure with your best friend, Jesus.

Key Truth for Chapter 14: Jesus is always with you as your forever friend, and He promises to guide you, help you, and welcome you into His eternal presence one day.

Activity Idea: My Promise from God

The Bible is full of God's promises to us. Find one of these verses (or another one you love) and write it out. This promise is for YOU.

✝"I am with you always, to the very end of the age." (Matthew 28:20)

✝"I can do all this through Him who gives me strength." (Philippians 4:13)

✝"For God so loved the world that He gave His one and only Son, that whoever believes in Him shall not perish but have eternal life." (John 3:16)

My Favorite Promise:

Drawing My Future with Jesus

What do you imagine it will be like to be with Jesus in heaven forever? Draw a picture of what you think it might look like, or draw yourself walking with Jesus now.

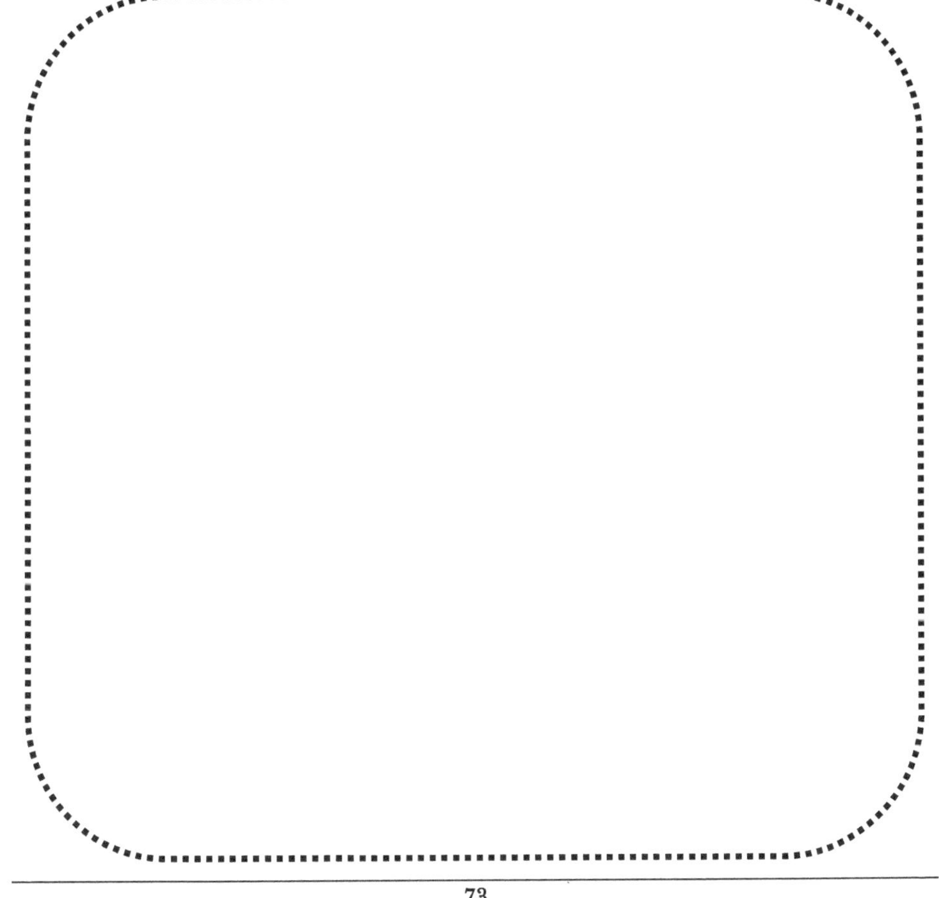

My Commitment Prayer:

You have reached the end of this book, but just the beginning of your journey with Jesus. You can pray this simple prayer:

Dear Jesus, Thank you for being my Forever Friend. Thank you for loving me, dying for my sins, and rising again. I want to walk with You every day. Please guide me, help me to obey You, and show me how to love others and share Your Good News. I look forward to being with You forever. Amen.

PART 2: BIBLE STUDY WORKBOOK FOR KIDS

Fun Activities and Simple Lessons to Grow Christian Faith Every Day

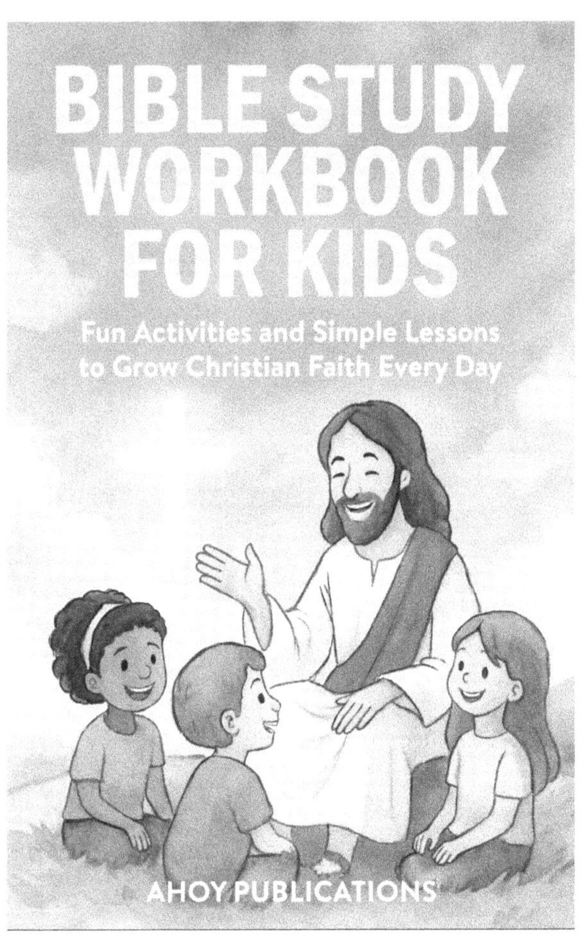

INTRODUCTION: READY FOR AN ADVENTURE?

Get ready for a journey through God's Word. This workbook is filled with stories, fun activities, and simple lessons that will help show you God's plan and your special place in it.

You'll explore important events from the Bible, from the very beginning of the world to Jesus' life and beyond. Each chapter is a new discovery, showing you more about God's love, His faithfulness, and His plan for everyone. You'll get to read exciting Bible passages, answer questions that make you think, and try out cool activities that help the lessons stick.

As you work through the chapters, you'll see how God's Word can guide your life every day and help your faith grow strong. So, open up your workbook, grab your Bible, and let's dive into this adventure together!

SECTION 1
GOD'S STORY BEGINS

CHAPTER 1: THE CREATOR GOD AND HIS PERFECT WORLD

Bible Focus: Genesis 1-2

Have you ever stopped to think about how everything around us got here? The towering mountains, the deep oceans, the tiny insects, and even the air we breathe: where did it all come from?

God's Word tells us that God made it all. He didn't use tools or need anyone's help; He simply spoke, and it happened! He created light, land, plants, animals, and finally, people.

He made Adam and Eve, giving them a special place in the Garden of Eden. And when God looked at everything He had made, He saw that it was truly good. He made you, too, and you are special to Him.

Main Point: God created everything good, including you as a unique part of His creation.

# LET'S GET CREATIVE!

Activity 1: My Perfect World Drawing

- ✝ Imagine a perfect world. What would it look like? What would be beautiful or peaceful in it?
- ✝ Use the space below or a separate piece of paper to draw your idea of a perfect world.

Activity 2: Nature Scavenger Hunt

✝ Go outside (or look out a window) and find **five things God created** in nature.

✝ Write down what you find below!

1. ____

2. ____

3. ____

4. ____

5. ____

Activity 3: Thank You God

✝ Think about something beautiful God made that you are thankful for.

____

____

✝ Write a short prayer of thanks for what you're thankful for.

____

____

____

____

____

📖 THINK AND DISCUSS

Reflect & Discuss:

✝ What does it mean that God created you?

____

____

✝ How can we care for His creation around us?

____

____

CHAPTER 2: WHEN THINGS WENT WRONG

Bible Focus: Genesis 3

In Chapter 1, we learned about God's perfect world. Something happened that changed everything. Adam and Eve were in a beautiful garden, and God gave them just one rule: do not eat from the *tree of the knowledge of good and evil.*

The serpent tricked Eve. It made her doubt God's Word and want what was forbidden. Eve ate the fruit, and then she gave some to Adam, and he ate it too.

Their choice broke their perfect relationship with God and brought pain and hardship. Their eyes were opened, they realized they were naked and they made coverings from fig leaves to cover themselves. They tried to hide from God, but God knew what happened.

He spoke to them about their choices and the consequences. Even though their choices had serious results, God still showed

His love by making clothes for them and by starting to put His rescue plan into action.

Main Point: Sin separates us from God, but God had a plan to make a way back to Him.

LET'S THINK ABOUT CHOICES!

Activity 1: Choices & Consequences Maze

✝ Imagine you're at the start of a path. Draw a simple maze below.

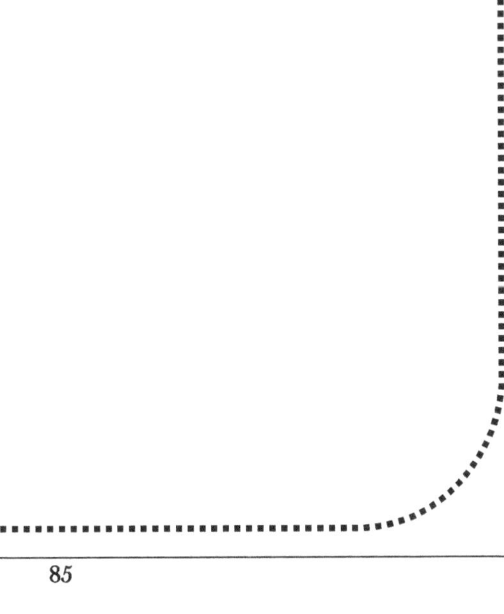

✝ At different turns, write "Good Choice" or "Wrong Choice."

✝ Show how a "Wrong Choice" leads to a less desirable outcome (like a dead end or a messy path), while a "Good Choice" leads to a clear and pleasant end.

Activity 2: Right or Wrong?

✝ Read each action below. Decide if it's a **Right Choice** or a **Wrong Choice**.

✝ Tick the correct box.

Action	Right Choice	Wrong Choice
Sharing your toys	[ ]	[ ]
Hitting a friend	[ ]	[ ]
Telling the truth	[ ]	[ ]
Taking something without asking	[ ]	[ ]
Helping someone in need	[ ]	[ ]

Activity 3: Why Choices Matter

✝ Think about a time you made a small choice that led to a big outcome. Maybe it was a good outcome, or maybe it wasn't.

✝ Briefly describe what happened and how it felt.

THINK AND DISCUSS

Reflect & Discuss:

   ✟ What is sin?

   ✟ Why does God care about our choices?

Reflect & Discuss:

CHAPTER 3: GOD'S PROMISE TO NOAH

Bible Focus: Genesis 6-9

After sin entered the world, things became very bad. People were doing many wrong things, and their thoughts were often evil. God saw how much wickedness was on the earth, and it grieved Him.

There was one person, Noah, who found favor in God's eyes. Noah walked with God.

God told Noah He was going to send a great flood to cover the earth and wipe out all living things. Because Noah trusted God, God gave him a way to be saved. He told Noah to build a large ark, a huge boat, and to take his family and animals onto the ark.

Noah obeyed God exactly as he was commanded, even though it was a very big and unusual task. He took seven pairs of clean animals and two of every unclean animal onto the ark.

When the flood came, the ark floated, protecting Noah, his family, and the animals. After many days on the water, Noah sent out a raven, and then a dove, to see if the waters had gone down. When the land was finally dry, they came out onto dry land.

God then made a promise: He would never again destroy all life on earth with a flood. As a sign of this promise, God put a rainbow in the sky. The rainbow reminds us that God is faithful and always keeps His Word.

Main Point: God is just, and He always keeps His promises.

 LET'S GET ACTIVE!

Activity 1: Building a Mini Ark

- ✝ Imagine you are Noah! How would you build the ark?
- ✝ Use LEGOs, blocks, craft sticks, or even draw a detailed picture of a large boat that could hold many animals. Use the space below for your drawing or notes.

Activity 2: Rainbow Promise Craft

✝ Draw a large rainbow.

✝ On each color of the rainbow, write or draw one promise you know God has made from the Bible. (For example: "I will never leave you," "He will forgive your sins," "Jesus is coming back," "He loves you.")

Activity 3: Finding Hope Word Search

✝ Find the words listed below in the puzzle (search for the words from left to right in the below sentences).

NOAHARKPRAINBOW
ROBEDIENCEHOPEPROMISE
MSOHOPEENAEIFAITH
TLSALVATIONEBOTS
FLOODSTORYWOR

Words to find:

✝ NOAH

✝ ARK

✝ FLOOD

✝ PROMISE

✝ RAINBOW

✝ FAITH

✝ OBEDIENCE

✝ HOPE

✝ SALVATION

✝ STORY

THINK AND DISCUSS

Reflect & Discuss:

✝ How does Noah's story show God's character?

____

____

✝ What promises do we find in God's Word today that give us hope?

____

____

SECTION 2
GOD CHOOSES A FAMILY

CHAPTER 4: A BIG FAMILY FOR A BIG GOD

Bible Focus: Genesis 12, 15, 22

After the flood, people began to spread out again, and many started to forget God. God had a plan to bring people back to Himself through one special family.

He chose a man named Abram (later called Abraham) who lived in a city called Ur. God told Abram to leave his home and travel to a new land that He would show him. God also made Abram an incredible promise: He would make Abram into a great nation, bless him, and through him, all the families on earth would be blessed.

Abram trusted God and obeyed, even though he didn't know exactly where he was going. He traveled with his wife, Sarai, and his nephew, Lot. God showed him the land of Canaan. Even though Abram and Sarai were old and had no children, God promised Abram that he would have more descendants than the stars in the sky!

Later, God changed Abram's name to Abraham and Sarai's name to Sarah, as a sign of this big promise. Even when they were very old, Abraham and Sarah had a son named Isaac.

God even tested Abraham's faith by asking him to offer his son Isaac, the son of the promise. Abraham was ready to obey, trusting that God would keep His word, even to raise Isaac from the dead. However, God stopped him, providing a ram as a sacrifice instead. Abraham's story shows us that God keeps His promises and wants us to trust Him fully.

Main Point: God chooses people for His plans and asks for our trust.

LET'S GET ACTIVE!

Activity 1: Star Promise Constellation

- ✝ God promised Abraham that his descendants would be as many as the stars.

- ✝ Draw a night sky below and draw many big stars. Inside some of the stars, write words or short phrases that remind you of God's promises (e.g., "God is with me," "Jesus loves me," "God forgives me"). Connect some stars to make your own "constellations of promises."

Activity 2: Trust Walk

✝ This activity needs a grown-up helper!

✝ Find a safe, clear space. Close your eyes (or wear a blindfold if a grown-up is guiding you safely) and let your grown-up guide you a few steps.

✝ Think about how it felt to trust them to lead you without seeing. How is trusting God similar?

Think about it:

✝ Was it easy or hard to trust your grown-up? Why?

✝ How does this help you understand what it means to trust God?

Activity 3: My Family Tree

✝ God promised Abraham a big family.

✝ Draw a simple family tree below with enough space for writing names, starting with yourself, then your family members. Think about who makes up your family!

 # THINK AND DISCUSS

Reflect & Discuss:

✝ What does it mean to trust God even when it's hard or when you don't understand everything?

____

____

✝ Can you think of a time when you had to trust someone even when you couldn't see what would happen next?

____

____

CHAPTER 5: GOD RESCUES HIS PEOPLE

Bible Focus: Exodus 1-14

Hundreds of years passed after Abraham. His family grew into many people, becoming the nation of Israel. They moved to Egypt, seeking food during a famine. At first, they were welcomed and lived well in the land of Goshen.

A new king came to power in Egypt. He did not know about Joseph, a descendant of Abraham who had been a powerful leader and God's helper in Egypt many years before, saving the country from a terrible famine.

This new king feared the Israelites because they were so many. He forced them into slavery, making their lives very hard. The Egyptians made the Israelites build cities and work long hours.

The Israelites cried out to God in their suffering. God heard their prayers and remembered His promise to Abraham. He decided it was time to rescue His people from slavery.

God chose a man named Moses for this important task. Moses had been saved as a baby from Pharaoh's orders to throw all Israelite boys in the Nile River to ensure they did not survive.

His mother put him in a basket and hid him in the Nile River. Pharaoh's own daughter found the baby and raised him in the palace as her own son.

He grew up in Pharaoh's palace but later fled to the desert. One day, God spoke to Moses from a burning bush that was not burning up in its fire. God told Moses to go to Pharaoh and demand that he let God's people go free. Moses felt afraid and unsure, but God promised to be with him and give him the words to say.

Moses and his brother Aaron went to Pharaoh. Pharaoh refused to let the Israelites go. So, God sent ten powerful plagues upon Egypt. These plagues showed God's power over Pharaoh and all of Egypt's false gods.

The last plague was the worst, bringing death to the firstborn sons of Egypt. God instructed the Israelites to put the blood of a lamb on their doorframes, offering protection. This event is called the Passover. It reminded them of God's protection.

Pharaoh finally let the Israelites go. God led them with a pillar of cloud by day and a pillar of fire by night. Pharaoh changed his mind and chased them with his army to the Red Sea. The Israelites were trapped with the sea in front and Pharaoh's army behind.

Moses lifted his staff, and God parted the Red Sea. The Israelites walked across on dry ground. Pharaoh's army tried to follow, but the waters crashed back, covering them. God completely rescued His people from slavery.

Main Point: God is powerful and always rescues His people from trouble. He wants us to be free!

 # LET'S GET ACTIVE!

Activity 1: Passover Meal Discussion

- ✝ The Passover meal was very important for the Israelites.
- ✝ With a grown-up, prepare a simple snack with symbolic elements (e.g., crackers for unleavened bread, grapes for wine/joy, a small herb for bitterness). Discuss what each item might represent in the Passover story.
- ✝ Draw a picture of a family celebrating Passover.

Activity 2: Red Sea Crossing

✝ Create a simple "Red Sea Crossing" obstacle course in a room or yard.

✝ You could use blankets or towels as the "water" and walk between them on a "dry path."

✝ Think about how amazing it must have been for the Israelites to walk through the sea!

Think about it:

✝ How did God show His power in this story?

____

____

✝ What is something God has helped you get through?

____

____

Activity 3: Freedom Chain

✝ On strips of paper, write or draw things that God frees us from (e.g., fear, sadness, bad choices, sin).

✝ Connect the strips to make a paper chain, showing how God's freedom connects many parts of our lives.

# THINK AND DISCUSS

Reflect & Discuss:

✝ How did God show His power in the story of the Exodus?

____

____

✝ How does Jesus set us free today?

____

____

____

CHAPTER 6: GOD'S RULES FOR LIFE

Bible Focus: Exodus 19-20

After God rescued His people from Egypt, He led them through the wilderness. He provided for them, giving them food called manna and water. He was always with them, guiding them by a cloud during the day and fire at night. God had a plan to teach His people how to live as His special family.

God led the Israelites to Mount Sinai. He called Moses up the mountain. There, God spoke to Moses and gave him special rules for His people to live by. These rules are called the Ten Commandments. God gave them because He loves His people. He wanted them to know how to live in a way that honors Him and shows love to others. The commandments show us what God is like, and they also show us that we cannot perfectly keep all of God's rules on our own.

The first four commandments teach us how to love God. They tell us to worship only Him, to honor His name, and to remember His special day of rest. The last six commandments teach us how to love our neighbors. They tell us to respect our parents, not to lie, not to steal, not to hurt others, and to be content with what we have.

Following these rules helps us live good lives and shows others what it means to follow God. The rules also show us that we all need God's help because no one can follow them perfectly. This points us to Jesus, who did follow God's rules perfectly.

Main Point: God gives us rules because He loves us and wants what's best. These rules also show us our need for Jesus.

 **LET'S GET ACTIVE!**

Activity 1: Commandment Match-Up

Draw a line from each commandment idea to what it tells us to do.

Commandment Idea	What it tells us to do
No other gods	[ ] Only worship God
Do not misuse God's name	[ ] Speak about God with respect
Remember the Sabbath day	[ ] Rest and honor God one day a week and keep it holy
Honor your father and mother	[ ] Listen to and respect your parents
Do not murder	[ ] Do not harm others
Do not steal	[ ] Do not take things that are not yours
Do not lie	[ ] Always tell the truth
Do not desire or wish for something eagerly	[ ] Be happy with what God has given you

Activity 2: Heart Check

✝ Be honest! Is it easy or hard to always follow all of God's rules? Why do you think that is?

✝ In the space below, draw a smiley face if it's easy or a thoughtful face if it's hard.

✝ Write a sentence about why you chose that face.

Activity 3: Showing Love

✝ God's rules help us show love to Him and to others.

✝ Draw a picture of someone showing love to God (like praying, singing, or reading the Bible) OR showing love to others (like sharing, helping, or being kind).

THINK AND DISCUSS

Reflect & Discuss:

✝ Are rules always bad? How do God's rules help us?

✝ How do God's rules help us understand more about Him and ourselves?

SECTION 3
GOD SENDS HIS KING

CHAPTER 7: THE PROMISED KING IS BORN

Bible Focus: Matthew 1-2, Luke 1-2

Many years passed after God gave His rules to Moses. God's people faced many challenges. Even through these times, God kept His promise to send a Savior. God's Word had many clues about this special King who would come to rescue His people.

God sent the angel Gabriel to a young woman named Mary. Gabriel told Mary she would have a baby, and this baby would be God's own Son. His name would be Jesus, and He would be King forever. Mary was engaged to a man named Joseph. Joseph was a good man. He also learned about God's plan for Jesus through an angel in a dream.

A new rule from the government meant everyone had to travel to their hometowns to be counted. Joseph and Mary traveled a long way to Bethlehem, Joseph's family town. The town was very crowded when they arrived. There was no room for them in any inn.

Mary gave birth to Jesus in a humble stable. She wrapped Him in cloths and laid Him in a manger, a feeding trough for animals. This was a simple beginning for the most important King ever.

That night, shepherds were in the fields nearby, watching their sheep. An angel of the Lord appeared to them. The angel told them not to be afraid. He announced the birth of the Savior, Christ the Lord, in Bethlehem. A whole group of angels then appeared, praising God and saying, "Glory to God in the highest heaven, and on earth peace to those on whom His favor rests."

The shepherds quickly went to Bethlehem. They found Mary, Joseph, and the baby Jesus, just as the angel had told them. They shared what they had heard and seen, and everyone who heard was amazed.

Some time later, wise men from the East also followed a special star. They traveled a long distance to find the new King. They worshipped Jesus and gave Him precious gifts: gold, frankincense, and myrrh. Jesus' birth showed that God kept His promise to send a Savior for all people.

Main Point: God kept His promise to send a Savior, Jesus, who is God with us.

 LET'S GET CREATIVE!

Activity 1: Nativity Scene Storytelling

- ✝ If you have a nativity set at home, use the figures to tell the story of Jesus' birth in your own words.
- ✝ If you don't have a set, you can draw your favorite part of the Christmas story below.

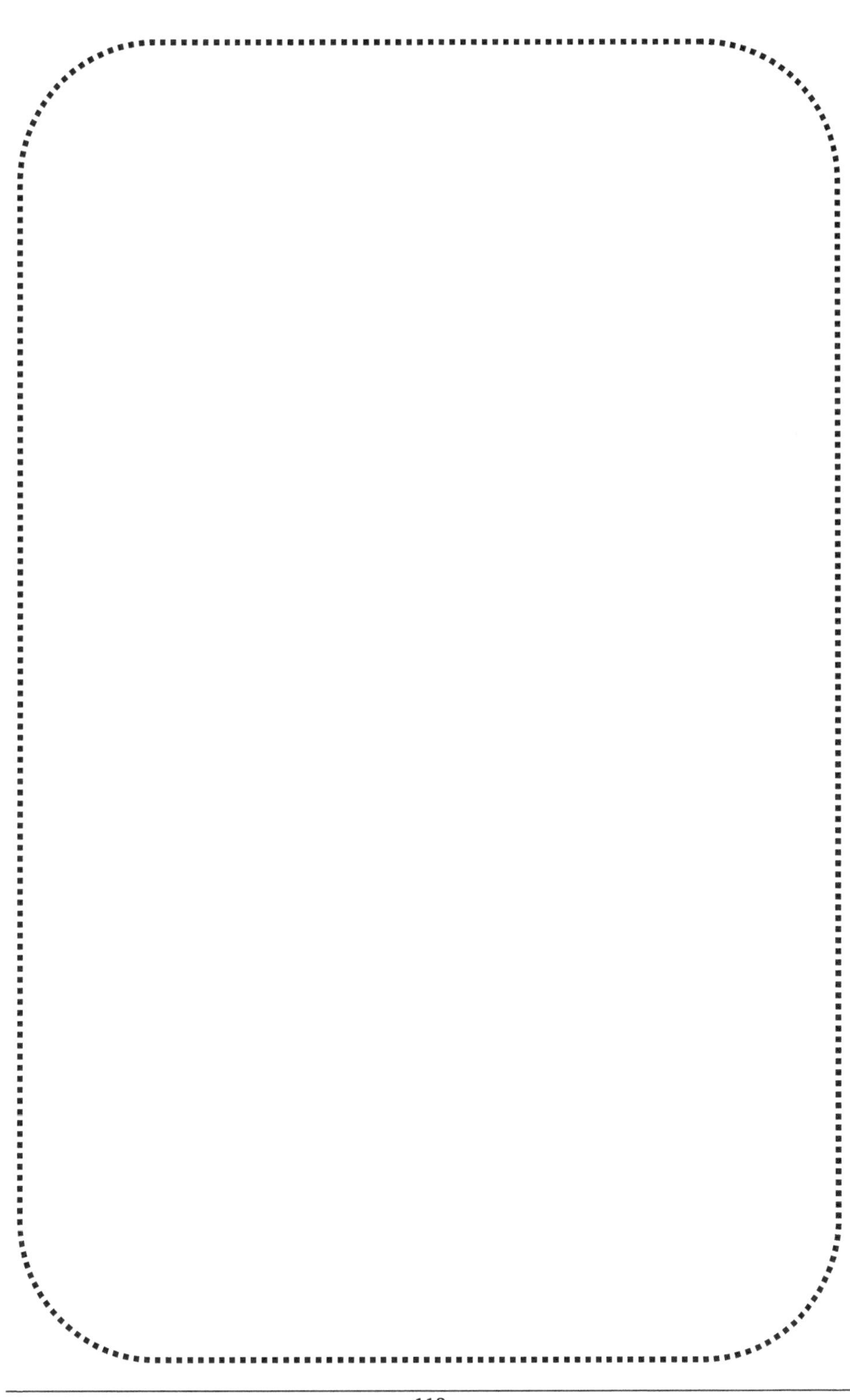

Activity 2: Gifts from Jesus

☩ When we receive a gift, it makes us happy. Jesus gave us the greatest gift when He came to earth!

☩ What gifts does Jesus give to us? List three gifts below. (Example: forgiveness, hope, love, peace)

1. ____

2. ____

3. ____

Activity 3: Christmas Song Fill-in

Fill in the missing words from this classic Christmas song.

"Silent Night"

Silent night, holy night, All is ____________, all is ______________. Round yon virgin Mother and Child, Holy infant so ______________ and mild, Sleep in heavenly ______________, Sleep in heavenly ______________.

(Words to choose from: calm, bright, tender, peace)

📖 THINK AND DISCUSS

Reflect & Discuss:

☩ Why is the birth of Jesus so important for God's people?

____

____

☩ What does it mean that Jesus is "God with us"?

____

____

CHAPTER 8: JESUS SHOWS GOD'S LOVE

Bible Focus: Selected parables and miracles

Jesus grew up. He began His work of teaching and showing God's love to the world. He called twelve special helpers, called disciples, to travel with Him and learn from Him. These disciples saw and heard everything Jesus did.

Jesus taught people about God's kingdom. He often used parables, which are simple stories with a deeper meaning. One time, He told a story about a kind helper, the Good Samaritan. This story showed how we should love everyone, even people who are different from us. Jesus also told a story about a lost son, often called the Prodigal Son. This story showed how much God loves us and welcomes us back, even when we make mistakes.

Jesus did many things that showed He was God's Son. He healed sick people. He gave sight to the blind and made people who could not walk, walk again. He even brought people back to life.

One time, a large crowd followed Jesus, and they became hungry. Jesus took five small loaves of bread and two fish. He prayed and shared the food. Thousands of people ate until they were full, with much food left over! This showed His power to provide for everyone. Jesus also showed His power over nature.

One day, He and His disciples were in a boat when a big storm came. The disciples were afraid. Jesus simply spoke to the wind and waves, and the storm became calm. Jesus' teachings and miracles proved that He was truly God's Son and He came to show us God's great love.

Main Point: Jesus came to show us what God is like – full of love, compassion, and power.

 LET'S GET ACTIVE!

Activity 1: Storytelling Skits

- ✝ Choose one of Jesus' miracles or parables (like the Good Samaritan, feeding the 5000, or calming the storm).
- ✝ With family or friends, act out the story! You can use simple props or just your imagination.
- ✝ What was the most important lesson in the story you chose?

Activity 2: Miracle Match

Draw a line from Jesus' miracle to what it showed about Him.

Jesus' Miracle   What it Showed About Jesus

Healing a sick   [   ] He has power over nature
person

Feeding thousands   [   ] He cares for people's needs and
of people   can provide

Calming a stormy   [   ] He has power over sickness and
sea   can make people well

Activity 3: Acts of Kindness Challenge

✝ Jesus showed love to others every day. How can you show God's love to someone this week?

✝ Think of one act of kindness you can do for a family member, friend, or neighbor. Write it down and try to do it!

My act of kindness: ______________________________

When I did it: __________________________________

How it felt: ___________________________________

📖✝ THINK AND DISCUSS

Reflect & Discuss:

✝ How did Jesus show love to others in the stories you read today?

____

____

____

✝ How can we show God's love to people around us in our
own lives?

CHAPTER 9: THE ULTIMATE SACRIFICE

Bible Focus: Matthew 26-27, Mark 14-15, Luke 22-23, John 18-19

Jesus taught and healed for about three years. Many people followed Him, listening to His words and seeing His miracles. Some religious leaders, however, did not like Him. They felt threatened by His words and actions, and they planned to get rid of Him.

Jesus knew His time on earth was coming to an end. He shared a final meal with His disciples. During this meal, He broke bread and poured wine. He told them to remember His body, broken for them, and His blood, poured out for the forgiveness of sins. This meal is often called the Last Supper.

After the meal, Jesus went to pray in the Garden of Gethsemane. Soldiers came and arrested Him. He was taken before powerful leaders for a trial. False accusations were made against Him. The leaders condemned Him to die, even though He had done nothing wrong.

Jesus was led away to be crucified. Crucifixion was a very painful way to die. They nailed Him to a wooden cross. Two criminals were crucified next to Him. Even on the cross, Jesus showed love and forgiveness. He asked God to forgive those who were hurting Him. Darkness covered the land while Jesus was on the cross.

Jesus died on the cross. His sacrifice paid the price for all the wrong things we have done. He died because He loves us so much. His death made a way for us to have a right relationship with God again. A soldier pierced His side, and blood and water came out. Jesus' friends took His body down from the cross. They placed Him in a tomb, a rock-cut grave. A large stone was rolled in front of the entrance.

Main Point: Jesus died for our sins because He loves us so much. This is the heart of God's redemptive story.

 LET'S GET ACTIVE!

Activity 1: Empty Cross Craft

✝ Draw a simple cross in the space below.

✝ Around the cross, write words or draw pictures that represent what Jesus did for you on the cross (e.g., love, forgiveness, new life, hope). The cross is a symbol of His sacrifice.

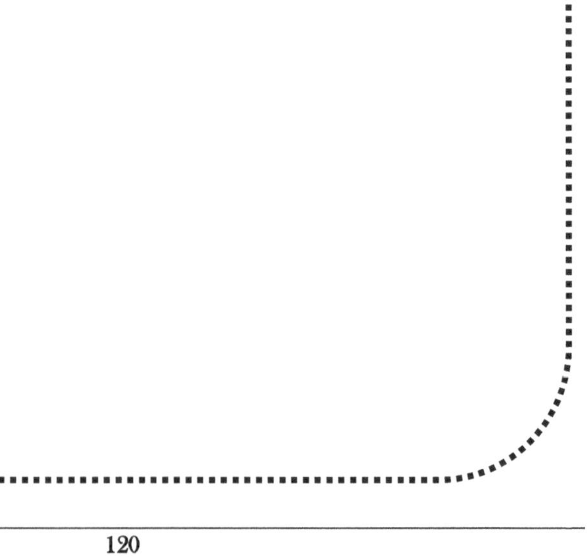

Activity 2: Forgiveness Chain

✝ On separate small strips of paper, write down one or two things you might have done wrong that you need God's forgiveness for.

✝ Then, take those strips and tear them or "break" them, symbolizing how Jesus' death breaks the power of sin and brings forgiveness.

Think about it:

✝ How does it feel to know Jesus took the punishment for our wrongs?

____

____

____

Activity 3: Love Sacrifices

✝ A "sacrifice" means giving up something for a greater purpose or out of love. Jesus made the ultimate sacrifice for us.

✝ Can you think of a small "love sacrifice" you could make for someone this week? (e.g., giving up screen time to play with a sibling, sharing your favorite toy, spending time helping a parent).

My love sacrifice idea: _______________________________

 **THINK AND DISCUSS**

Reflect & Discuss:

✝ What did Jesus do for us on the cross?

____

____

____

____

✝ How does Jesus' death change everything for us?

CHAPTER 10: THE KING LIVES!

Bible Focus: Matthew 28, Luke 24, John 20-21, Acts 1

Jesus' body was placed in a tomb, a cave-like grave. A large stone was rolled in front of the entrance. Guards were placed outside to keep watch. Many people thought Jesus' story was over.

On the third day after Jesus died, something wonderful happened. Early in the morning, Mary Magdalene and other women went to the tomb. They planned to prepare Jesus' body with spices. They arrived to find the large stone rolled away.

The tomb was empty! An angel was there. The angel told them not to be afraid. He announced that Jesus was not there; He had risen from the dead, just as He said He would.

The women ran to tell the disciples the news. At first, the disciples found it hard to believe. Peter and John ran to the tomb and saw it was empty. They saw the grave clothes lying there. Later, Jesus appeared to His disciples many times.

He showed them His hands and His side. He ate with them and talked with them. This proved to them that He was truly alive. Jesus conquered death! His resurrection showed that He truly is the Son of God and that His sacrifice on the cross worked perfectly.

Jesus stayed on earth for 40 days after He rose from the dead. He continued to teach His disciples about God's kingdom. One day, He led His disciples to the Mount of Olives.

As they watched, Jesus was lifted up into the sky and a cloud took Him out of their sight. This is called His ascension. Angels appeared and told the disciples that Jesus would come back in the same way He left. Jesus is now in heaven, preparing a place for those who believe in Him. His resurrection gives us hope for new life too.

Main Point: Jesus conquered death! He is alive, and because of Him, we can have a new life.

LET'S GET ACTIVE!

Activity 1: Joyful Shout!

✝ The resurrection of Jesus is the best news ever! It's a reason to celebrate.

✝ Think of something that makes you want to shout with joy. Maybe it's a birthday, a holiday, or good news.

✝ In the space below, draw a picture of yourself or someone else making a joyful shout!

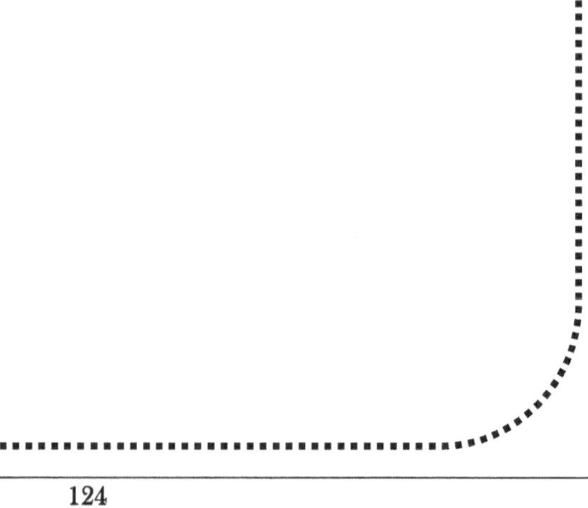

Activity 2: New Life Seed Planting

✝ Just as Jesus' resurrection brought new life, plants grow from seeds to new life.

✝ Get a small seed (like a bean or flower seed), a tiny pot or cup, and some soil. Plant the seed.

✝ As you water and watch it grow, remember that Jesus gives us new life when we believe in Him.

Think about it:

✝ How is a seed growing into a plant like new life in Jesus?

Activity 3: Good News Map

✝ Before Jesus went to heaven, He told His followers to share the Good News about Him with everyone.

✝ Draw a circle below to represent the world. Color in countries or places where you know people are sharing the Good News about Jesus. You can also draw lines from yourself to places you wish the Good News could go.

 # THINK AND DISCUSS

Reflect & Discuss:

✝ What does it mean that Jesus is alive?

____

____

✝ What difference does Jesus' resurrection make in our lives today?

____

____

SECTION 4
GOD'S SPIRIT AND OUR NEW LIFE

CHAPTER 11: GOD'S SPIRIT COMES!

Bible Focus: Acts 2

After Jesus went back to heaven, His disciples gathered together in Jerusalem. They were waiting, just as Jesus had told them. Jesus promised He would send a Helper, God's Spirit, to be with them and give them power.

Ten days after Jesus went to heaven, a special day called Pentecost arrived. The disciples were all together in one place. Suddenly, a sound like a strong wind filled the whole house where they were sitting. They saw what looked like tongues of fire that rested on each of them.

All of them were filled with the Holy Spirit. They began to speak in other languages that they had not learned before. People from many different countries were in Jerusalem for the feast of Pentecost. They heard the disciples speaking in their own languages. Everyone was amazed and wondered what was happening.

Peter, one of Jesus' disciples, stood up and explained. He told the crowd about Jesus, how He died for sins and rose again. He told them God sent His Spirit just as Jesus had promised. Peter invited them to believe in Jesus and turn from their wrong ways.

Many people believed Peter's message that day. About three thousand people became followers of Jesus and were baptized. This was the start of the church, God's family on earth.

The early followers of Jesus lived together and formed deep bonds with Jesus and each other. They learned from the apostles (Jesus' first followers), shared meals, and prayed together often. God's Spirit helped them. God's Spirit still lives in believers today. He helps us understand God's Word, guides us, and gives us power to live for God and tell others about Jesus.

Main Point: God sent His Holy Spirit to live in us, help us, and empower us to share His story.

 LET'S GET ACTIVE!

Activity 1: Wind Catcher

✝ The Holy Spirit's coming was described like a rushing wind. Wind is powerful, but you can't see it, only its effects!

✝ You can make a simple wind catcher by decorating a paper plate or a piece of cardboard. Cut strips from the bottom and attach ribbons or strings. Hang it up and watch how the air moves it. This reminds us of the Spirit's unseen power.

Activity 2: Gift Giving Charades

✝ The Holy Spirit gives each of us gifts so we can serve God and help others.

✝ With family or friends, play a game of charades. Act out simple abilities like "teaching," "helping," "singing," "listening," or "caring." See if others can guess what you're doing. This reminds us that we each have different ways to serve God.

Think about it:

✝ What is one way you think the Holy Spirit helps you or others?

____

____

Activity 3: Prayer Partner

✝ The Holy Spirit helps us pray.

✝ Think of someone you can pray for this week: a friend, a family member, a teacher. Write their name below.

✝ Make a plan to pray for them each day this week, asking the Holy Spirit to guide your prayers.

My Prayer Partner: ______________________________________

What I will pray for them: ______________________________

📖 THINK AND DISCUSS

Reflect & Discuss:

✝ How does the Holy Spirit help us today?

____

____

____

____

✝ What does it mean to be "filled with the Holy Spirit"?

____

____

____

____

CHAPTER 12: LIVING AS GOD'S CHILDREN

Bible Focus: Galatians 5:22-23

When we trust in Jesus and God's Spirit comes to live in us, our lives begin to change. We become God's children, part of His family. God's Spirit helps us grow in ways that show we belong to Him and are following Jesus.

God's Word tells us about the "fruit of the Spirit". Think of a fruit tree: it grows good fruit when it is healthy and cared for. In the same way, as God's Spirit works in us, good qualities grow in our lives. These qualities are like the fruit of our faith.

The Bible lists these qualities: love, joy, peace, patience, kindness, goodness, faithfulness, gentleness, and self-control.

What do these mean?

☩ **Love** means caring deeply for God and others, wanting what is best for them.

- ✝ **Joy** is a deep happiness that comes from God, even when things are hard around us.
- ✝ **Peace** is a calm feeling in our hearts and minds, trusting God no matter what happens.
- ✝ **Patience** means waiting calmly, being slow to get angry, and not giving up easily.
- ✝ **Kindness** is being friendly, thoughtful, and helpful to everyone.
- ✝ **Goodness** means doing what is right, being honest, and having a good heart.
- ✝ **Faithfulness** means being dependable and true to God and your promises.
- ✝ **Gentleness** means being soft-spoken and careful with others, not rough or mean.
- ✝ **Self-control** means being able to manage your actions, words, and feelings.

These qualities are not things we can make happen by just trying harder on our own. They are grown in us by the Holy Spirit as we spend time with God, read His Word, and choose to follow Him. We show the world what God is like when these good qualities grow in us.

Main Point: When we follow Jesus, God helps us grow good qualities that show His love to others.

 # LET'S GET CREATIVE!

Activity 1: Fruit Salad Qualities

✝ Draw a large fruit bowl below.

✝ Draw different kinds of fruit inside it. On each piece of fruit, write one of the "Fruit of the Spirit" qualities (love, joy, peace, patience, kindness, goodness, faithfulness, gentleness, self-control).

✝ Color in your fruit salad!

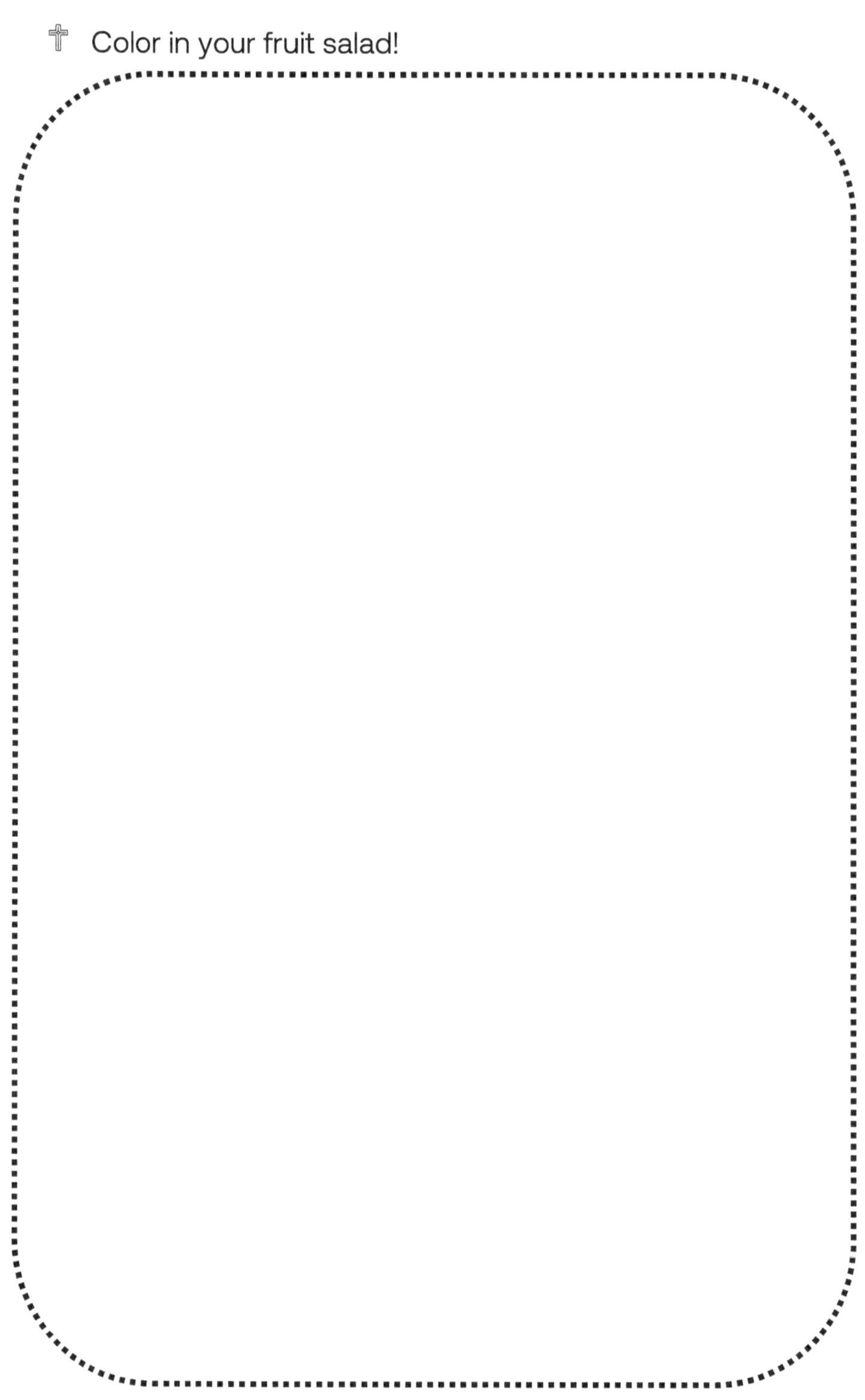

Activity 2: Showing Love Scenarios

Read each short story below. How could you show one of the "Fruit of the Spirit" qualities in that situation? Write your answer.

1. Your younger sibling/cousin keeps asking you to play, but you want to finish your game.

    ○ I could show **Patience** by: _______________________

    ○ I could show **Kindness** by: _______________________

2. Someone at school says something mean about you.

    ○ I could show **Self-control** by: _______________________

    ○ I could show **Gentleness** by: _______________________

Activity 3: Kindness Challenge

✝ Choose one person you know (a family member, friend, neighbor, or classmate).

✝ Think of one small act of kindness you can do for them this week to show God's love.

✝ Write down your plan and then try to do it!

    My kindness challenge: _______________________________

    ____

    When I did it: _______________________________________

    How it felt: ____

📖 THINK AND DISCUSS

Reflect & Discuss:

✝ Which "fruit of the Spirit" quality do you want God to help you grow more of? Why?

    ____

    ____

    ____

✝ How can showing these good qualities help others see what God is like?

CHAPTER 13: SHARING THE GOOD NEWS

Bible Focus: Matthew 28:18-20, Acts 1:8

When Jesus was about to go back to heaven, He gave His followers an important job. He told them to go everywhere in the world and tell people the Good News about Him. He said, "You will be my witnesses... to the ends of the earth." This job is called the Great Commission.

The first followers of Jesus took this job seriously. They traveled to many places. They told everyone about Jesus, how He lived, died, and rose again to save them from their sins. God's Spirit gave them power and courage to speak even when it was hard. The church began to grow as more and more people heard and believed.

What is the Good News? It is the message that God loves us so much He sent Jesus, His Son. Jesus died on the cross to take the punishment for our wrong choices (our sins). He came back to life, showing He beat death and sin. Anyone who believes in Jesus and trusts Him can have a new life with God and live with Him forever.

We are all called to share this Good News. We might not travel to faraway countries like some missionaries do. Missionaries are people who dedicate their lives to sharing Jesus in new places and cultures.

We can share the Good News right where we are, every day. We can do this with our words, telling others about what Jesus has done for us and who He is. We can also share through our actions, showing God's love by being kind, helpful, and fair to everyone.

We can tell our own story of how Jesus changed our lives. Sharing the Good News is like sharing the best gift ever. It helps others know about God's love and gives them a chance to join God's family too. It is a way to be part of God's big plan to reach the world.

Main Point: We are called to share the Good News of Jesus with everyone, through our words and our actions.

 LET'S GET ACTIVE!

Activity 1: Good News Reporter

- ✝ Imagine you are a reporter for the best news in the world!
- ✝ Write a newspaper headline and a very short report about the Good News of Jesus.

Headline: ____

Report:

____

____

____

____

____

____

Activity 2: My Witness Story

✝ A "witness" tells what they have seen or heard. You have a story about what you know about Jesus!

✝ In the space below, write three short sentences that show important parts of your journey with God or what you believe about Jesus.

1. ____

2. ____

3. ____

Activity 3: Prayer for the World

✝ The Great Commission tells us to go to the "ends of the earth".

✝ Look at a map or globe. Pick one country or group of people you've never heard of before.

✝ Pray for the people in that place, that they would hear the Good News of Jesus. Write down the place you prayed for.

I prayed for: ____

 **THINK AND DISCUSS**

Reflect & Discuss:

✝ What is the "Good News" in your own words?

____

____

____

✝ How can you share the Good News with someone this week, in a simple way?

____

____

____

CHAPTER 14: FOREVER WITH GOD

Bible Focus: Revelation 21-22, John 14:1-3, Acts 1:11

We have learned about God's story from the very beginning. We saw how God created a perfect world, how sin entered and broke things, and how God sent Jesus to make things right. God's story does not end there. It moves towards a joyful forever.

God has a wonderful future planned for everyone who believes in Jesus. We will live forever with Him in a perfect place. The Bible talks about a new heaven and a new earth where God will live with His people. It tells us what this place will be like.

In heaven, there will be no more sadness, no more crying, no more pain, and no more death. All the bad things will be gone forever. God Himself will be there with His people, and they will see His face. We will worship Him and enjoy being with Him perfectly, in a place without any sin or brokenness.

Jesus also made a promise before He went back to heaven. Christ said He would come again! We do not know the exact day or time when He will return, according to His own words, even He doesn't know, only the Father. We live with hope and excitement, looking forward to His return. When Jesus comes back, He will make all things new. He will gather all His children to live with Him forever in His perfect kingdom. This is the great promise for everyone who trusts in Jesus.

Knowing that we will live forever with God changes how we live today. It makes us want to grow closer to Him, obey Him, and share His Good News with others. We can live each day with joy and peace, knowing our true home is with God and that He is preparing a place for us.

Main Point: Our forever home is with God, and Jesus is coming back to make all things new.

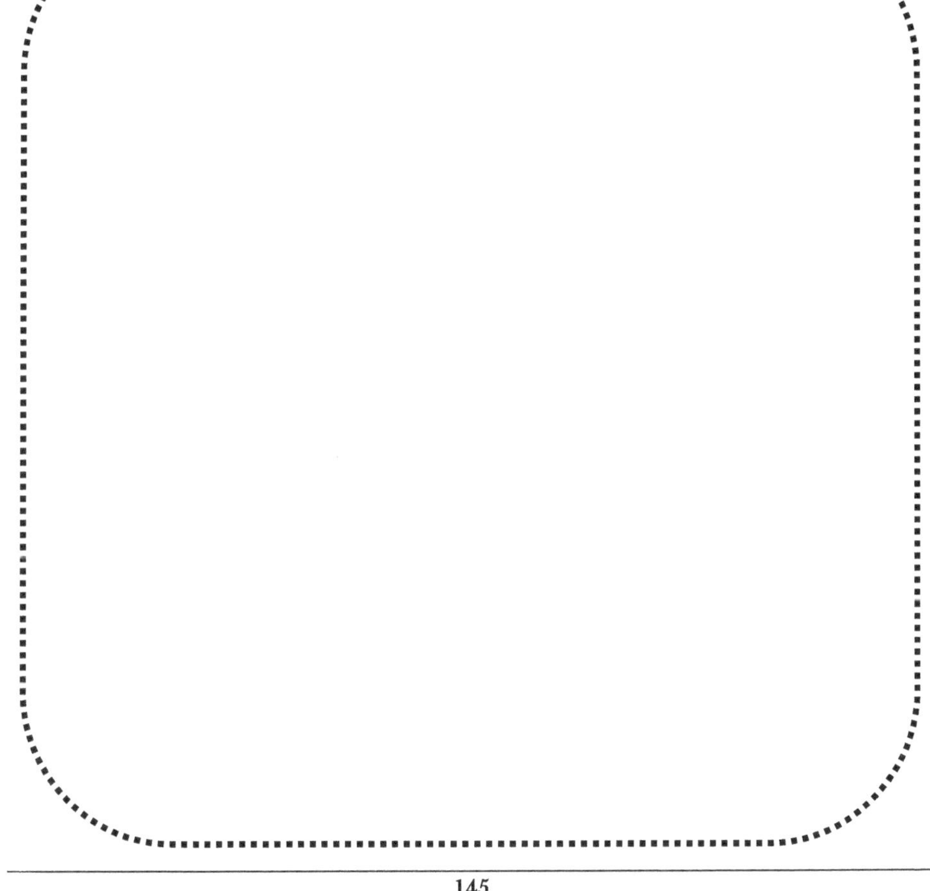 LET'S GET CREATIVE!

Activity 1: Heavenly Home Drawing

✝ The Bible describes heaven as a place with no tears or pain, where God lives with His people, and there's a river of life.

✝ In the space below, draw your idea of what a "perfect forever home with God" might look like. What makes it special?

Activity 2: Waiting with Hope Checklist

✝ We are waiting for Jesus to come back! While we wait, what are some things we can do to live for Him?

✝ Check off the things you can do to live with hope while waiting for Jesus:

[   ] Read my Bible

[   ] Pray to God

[   ] Help others

[   ] Tell someone about Jesus

[   ] Be kind and loving

[   ] Thank God for His promises

Activity 3: Forever Friends

✝ In heaven, we will be with God and with all who believe in Jesus.

✝ Write down the names of people you know (family, friends, church members) whom you hope to share eternity with in heaven. You can also draw pictures of them!

 # THINK AND DISCUSS

Reflect & Discuss:

☩ What part of being "forever with God" are you most excited about?

____

____

____

____

☩ How does knowing Jesus is coming back change how you live your life today?

____

____

____

____

CONCLUSION: YOUR PLACE IN GOD'S STORY

You have now finished a wonderful journey through God's big story! We started with how God created everything perfectly and how sin came into the world. We saw God's plan unfold, from His promises to Abraham and Noah, to His rescue of His people from Egypt.

You discovered how God gave His rules for living and how He sent His Son, Jesus, the promised King. You learned about Jesus' birth, His life, His powerful miracles, His loving teachings, and His great sacrifice on the cross. We celebrated His resurrection, when He conquered death! You learned how God sent His Holy Spirit to live in all who believe, helping us grow closer to God.

We thought about how we can share the good news of Christ's sacrifice and resurrection with others. You also looked forward to the wonderful promise of living forever with God in a new heaven and new earth.

God's story is still being written, and you are part of it! The Bible is full of truth and life. Keep reading your Bible to learn more about God and His plans. Keep talking to God in prayer, telling Him what's on your heart and listening for His guidance.

Let God's Holy Spirit guide you as you live each day. Share God's love with those around you, through your words and actions. Remember, God loves you very much, and He wants to walk with you every step of your life.

Keep seeking Him. Your adventure with God is neverending.

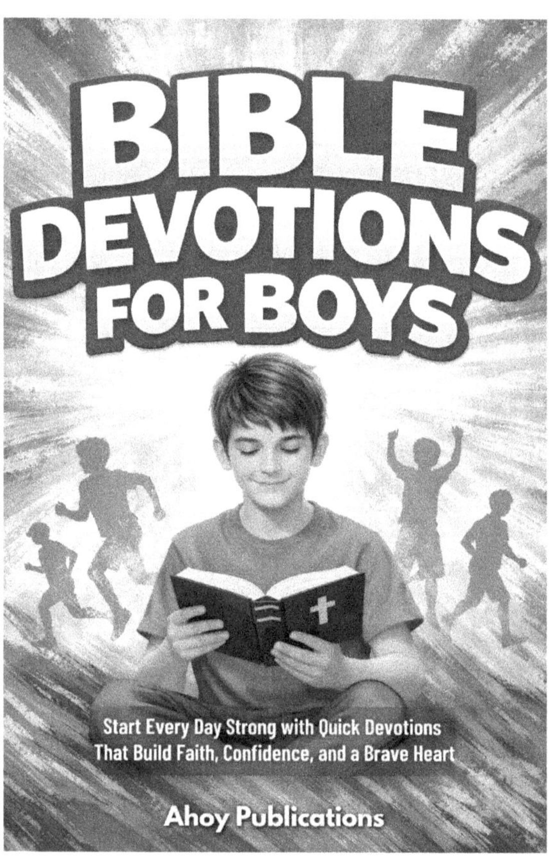

BIBLE
DEVOTIONS
FOR BOYS
Start Every Day Strong with Quick Devotions
That Build Faith, Confidence, and a Brave Heart
Ahoy Publications

WELCOME ABOARD, CHECK OUT THIS LIMITED-TIME FREE BONUS!

Ahoy, reader! Welcome to the Ahoy Publications family, and thanks for snagging a copy of this book! Since you've chosen to join us on this journey, we'd like to offer you something special.

Check out the link below for a FREE e-book filled with delightful facts about American History.

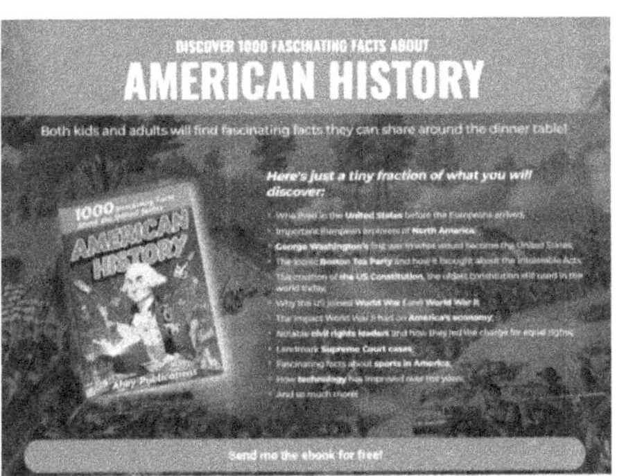

But that's not all - you'll also have access to our exclusive email list with even more free e-books and insider knowledge. Well, what are ye waiting for? Click the link below to join and set sail toward exciting adventures in American History.

Access your bonus here

https://ahoypublications.com/

Or, Scan the QR code!